BY HAND

BOOKS BY JOHN COYNE AND TOM HEBERT:

THIS WAY OUT: Alternatives to College

BY HAND: A Guide to Schools and Careers in Crafts

BY HAND

A Guide to Schools and Careers in Crafts

JOHN COYNE & TOM HEBERT

A SUNRISE BOOK
E. P. DUTTON & CO., INC., NEW YORK 1974

For Our Nieces and Nephews

Library of Congress Cataloging in Publication Data
Coyne, John
  By hand; a guide to schools and careers in crafts

  Bibliography: p.
    1. Handicraft—Study and teaching—Directories.
2. Artisans. I. Hebert, Tom, joint author.
II. Title.
TT12.C69 1974   745.5   73–18022

Published simultaneously in Canada
by Clarke, Irwin & Company Limited, Toronto and Vancouver

ISBN: 0-87690-119-4 (cloth)
ISBN: 0-87690-120-8 (paper)

Outerbridge & Lazard, a subsidiary of
E. P. Dutton & Co., Inc.

ACKNOWLEDGMENTS

For their advice and assistance we would like to thank craftsmen Marian and Don Beil; Wendy Ross of the National Parks Service; Carolyn Hecker of Smithsonian Associates; Lloyd Herman of the Renwick Gallery of the Smithsonian Institution; Dave Sennema of the National Endowment for the Arts; William R. Seymour of the Department of Agriculture; Andrea Sanford Schmertz and Amy Hardy of the Appalachian Regional Commission; Richard Mower of Montgomery College; Caroline Ramsay of the Office of Economic Opportunity; Bill Brown of Penland Crafts School; Garnette Johnson of the Handweavers Guild of America; the Research Department of the American Crafts Council; and the National Association of Schools of Art.

CONTENTS

PART I

PART II

PART III

PART IV

PART I

WORLD OF CRAFTS

In doing research for our book *This Way Out: Alternatives to College,* we discovered a substantial subculture of college-age men and women involved with crafts. For the most part these students had given up academic education to work with their hands. Many were learning on their own, in craft cooperatives, through private lessons, or by taking courses at craft centers. And they were not alone. The interest in crafts has spread to other adults. Professional people, housewives, bureaucrats, and others, were all doing crafts.

It was apparent, however, that a guide to the craft schools and centers was needed, for many people did not know where they could go to learn a skill, or how to go about making a living from their craft. The interest in crafts is more than an avocation for many people. Students are learning skills in order to make a living.

This growing interest in crafts over the last fifteen years can be best termed spectacular. College programs, for one example, have grown from 16 in 1962 to over 750 today. There have been other dramatic indications of growth: in 1973 the League of New Hampshire Craftsmen annual craft fair grossed close to $175,000. Ten years ago that show would have been lucky to make $35,000.

Donald L. Page, executive secretary-treasurer of the West Virginia Artists and Craftsmens Guild, says that the arts and crafts program in West Virginia has grown over 3,000 percent since 1963. He estimates that the combined income of some 2,000 participating craftsmen in the West Virginia fairs (over 55) has shown an increase in sales from $7,500 in 1963 to $140,000 in 1973.

According to Donald Wyckoff, executive vice-president of the American Crafts Council, "there has been steady growth all across the country. No matter what criterion you use—sales volume or number of craft shows or amount of participation—this year has been the best we've ever had. And last year was the best before that, and so on. Just steady growth."

William R. Seymour, chairman of the Interagency Crafts Committee of the U.S. government, sees the revival of crafts as a "sleeping giant." Seymour, who is the craft specialist for the Farmer Cooperative Service of the Department of Agriculture, believes that the income from crafts overall in 1973 totaled over $15 million.

Rose Slivka, editor-in-chief of *Craft Horizons,* writes, "the craftsman has demonstrated that there is an economic base . . . his production, limited in order to assure personal control of quality, will not earn him a million dollars, but simply a modest living for himself and his family."

But economics is not the only reason so many people are now turning to crafts for a new way of life. Crafts are being seen as leisure-time activities, creative hobbies, therapy, and in areas like Appalachia, potential industry. Yet more than any of these, crafts are seen as the way to a new life, a lifestyle other than a nine-to-five job. And a life that will fulfill economic, social and cultural needs.

Charles Counts, a potter whose workshop is located in Rising Fawn, on Lookout Mountain in north Georgia, writing in *Appalachia,* the magazine of the Appalachian Regional Commission, explains why ceramics is still popular and why people turn to the craft.

I believe the craft has persisted because of its unique human value, because of the dark mystery of taking soft, formless, commonly available clay and making it into a firm vessel which offers both beauty and utility. In our times an increasing number of young people have turned to pottery making as a means of art expression and as a way to satisfy their urge to make something really well.

Ceramics is the most popular of the crafts—it is estimated that 80 percent of all craftsmen are potters—but the growth in other crafts is also significant. Today people are making a living and a lifestyle by working in metals, fabrics, glass, leather and wood.

To understand the recent growth in crafts and the newly rediscovered need people have for things "handmade," it's necessary to understand something of the history of handcrafted items. Andrea Sanford Schmertz in a special study for the Appalachian Regional Commission describes this history and how it relates to the United States.

The pre-Industrial Age produced by hand items for everyday use and adornment: handicrafts were expressions of the people, their times and culture. With the widespread use of machines for production of functional articles, handicrafts lost their place as useful commodities and were delegated to production in backward areas and by isolated peoples.

As the Industrial Revolution grew, idealistic efforts to counteract the effect of machinery and machine-made goods on man were made. The Arts and Crafts Movement in nineteenth-century England personified in the works of William Morris and his followers in one example. The Bauhaus in Germany did not attempt to revive crafts as Morris did, but sought to reach new concepts of form and design through the use of craft skills for machine-made products. The present-day multimillion-dollar crafts industry of Denmark grew out of a similar search for new designs and forms based on craft traditions but for contemporary society.

The Arts and Crafts Movement of England has had significance for Appalachia. Arts and crafts were employed by misssionaries and educators in the last century in order to provide a cash income for mountain people. When it was discovered that a market for hand-crafted products could be found, groups were developed to serve this market which idealized hand production over machines.

Such attempts to make crafts an industry has continued, especially during the late 1960s and early 1970s as the Office of Economic Opportunity supplied grants of an estimated $12 million for craft development in depressed areas of the United States. Also the Department of Agriculture and its Farmer's Cooperative Administration has lent in recent years over $300,000 to craft associations, and the National Endowment for the Arts through its state offices has given money to individuals and guilds in support of craft activities.

Much of this assistance, according to Andrea Sanford Schmertz, has not been an advantage to the craftsman and the crafts industry. "The market has been overcrowded with low-quality crafts. . . . Many craft enterprises have failed because of an unrealistic assessment of the craft market and production. . . . Crafts which grew out of the cultural needs of an earlier time have been revived for economic enterprises without the realization that many can never be commercial products."

Besides these problems, craftsmen themselves are divided—the folk or traditional craftsman, the contemporary university-trained craftsman, the artist-craftsman, the designer-craftsman, the artisan or craft worker and the hobbyist have trouble communicating with each other. Each feels that his craft, and approach to crafts, is the only way, therefore organizing the total industry is extremely difficult.

Yet with all of these troubles and factionalisms, the world of crafts continues to expand. People of all ages are finding, as teacher and potter Paulus Berensohn writes, "their way with clay." People are learning again how to forge, blow glass, work in fabrics; they are becoming silversmiths, weavers, joiners. They are becoming skilled.

And by gaining these skills, they are also gaining a little better control of their lives, learning how to live well, but in a different way. For working in crafts makes a person tone down his or her life, helps a person reduce the complexities of living. A stranger need only visit the Penland School of Crafts—an old, traditional crafts school in the hills of northwestern North Carolina—to sense the tranquility of the place and the world that crafts can provide. "There is something about the material of crafts," William Brown, Director of Penland, has said, "that keeps a person truthful."

Genuine craftsmen don't view crafts as an avocation but as a career. They want to structure their lives around the production of handmade items.

This is not easily done. The number of full-time craftsmen is limited. The majority of craftsmen earn a large part of their living by teaching crafts. And many of the well-known craftsmen earn very good livings from lecturing and doing short courses in their field.

To understand how to make a living from crafts, one should know the skill classifications. Charles Counts in his excellent study *Encouraging American Craftsmen,* a report for the Interagency Crafts Committee of the federal government, has defined four types of craft persons.

> *Craftworker:* A craftworker is one employed to do any sort of work in relation to a craft enterprise. He may stack the pottery kilns, prepare yarns and fibers for weaving, or secure and dress the wood for furniture. . . . A craftworker is generally trained as an apprentice, if at all, although this system is not so widely used as it might be or so highly developed in this country as it is in many foreign countries. . . .
>
> *Traditional Craftsman:* A traditional or folk craftsman is an individual usually responsible for his own products, who works in a home or a community where skills are handed down from generation to generation. . . . Actually there are very few unspoiled traditional craftsmen left in the United States. They exist only in remote areas such as in out-of-way Indian reservations or isolated parts of the southern mountains.
>
> *Artist-craftsman:* An artist-craftsman is a craftsman who creates his own designs and generally makes one-of-a-kind products, usually in his own shop or studio. He is concerned with his own satisfaction as an artist, and his work may become non-utilitarian and tend toward sculpture or painting. The artist-craftsman is frequently highly educated. He has usually attended a college or university which offers courses in applied arts or craft school where he studies the principles

of design and the history of art, thereby gaining an understanding of the cultural significance of the crafts. . . . In some cases, the artist-craftsman is self-taught and occasionally achieves a fair degree of competency by this means.

Designer-craftsman: A designer-craftsman is an artist-craftsman who creates designs for others to execute. He may employ several craftworkers in a shop of his own or employ workers elsewhere. . . . Or again, he may design for a handcraft industry, in which case he might be called an industrial designer. The work of the designer-craftsman combines all that is inherent in the definition of design with all that is meant by the word craft. . . . The word "design" implies exploration, experimentation, and originality, so that the designer-craftsman, like the artist-craftsman, is essentially an artist.

It is the last two types, *artist-craftsman* and *designer-craftsman,* that interest us. These are the people who are making their livings from crafts. How they go about it and where they have learned their skills is what this section is all about.

FOUR WASHINGTON CRAFTSMEN

These craftsmen are from Washington, D.C. We selected them to show the variety of work possibilities in crafts, and how some people have found a way of making a living from their skill. These job opportunities could be duplicated anywhere in the United States.

Thurid and Noel Clark, weaver and potter
Bill Cook, metalsmith
Solveig Cox, potter
Ron Goodman, weaver

THURID AND NOEL CLARK

About one hour from Washington on the Appalachian Trail and next to the Gathland State Park is Tollhouse Craftsmen, a craft shop, studio and gallery owned by Thurid and Noel Clark, two ex-Washingtonians who left the city and their Potomac Park suburban lives to move their family onto a half acre of cleared land that overlooks beautiful Pleasant Valley. They "dropped out" to become full-time craftsmen.

When they quit the city Noel was a successful Washington contractor who threw pots only as a hobby and Thurid was a housewife and well-known weaver. Both are in their mid-thirties. Thurid is a strong, handsome woman, Germanic-looking, who dresses simply and likes, she says, to live simply. Noel is short, stocky, quick to smile and make people at ease. He has developed a full black beard and wears steel-framed glasses, country-like.

Tollhouse is built of oak and walnut planks that have been left to age naturally. It is a plain building, rustic, with the main floor devoted to the display of crafts. Downstairs are the studios, separated and connected by a door. "We like to work alone," Thurid explained while showing me through the studios. "I need quiet to concentrate on color selection and design, and Noel likes to work with music playing."

We did the interview in a small room off the shop that the Clarks had set up as a lounge. They spend a lot of time in Tollhouse and have made it as comfortable as their home. Their real home is across the yard, an old Civil War house that had been the original tollhouse.

We began by asking them if there had been problems with having their studios so close to the shop.

"Well, some people come expecting to see craftsmen at work," Noel explained. "You get the feeling they think craftsmen are like caged animals, something to look at. What we're trying to do is sell a pot, not because someone has seen it being made, but because it's beautiful."

"A lot," Thurid added, "come because they want to see the weaver work and we tell them no you can't see the weaver work and, of course, they're very angry. It seems most people feel that if someone has a skill they'd feel so great about showing it off. They really can't understand that you wouldn't want to sit there and weave for them. But then I'm very much into the creativity of it and I just can't have anyone talking to me while I work. People don't understand this."

"Beyond the fact that they come to see the weaver work, come to see the potter," we asked, "do they come for other reasons out from Washington and Baltimore?"

"Oh, well, yes," Noel said, "we offer things that aren't available elsewhere. This is the only place they can come to buy Thurid's weaving, for one. Also the atmosphere in our shop is different from the city, and the Appalachian Trail is here . . . also, we're open on Sundays."

"And information," Thurid added, "people come and say

I've just started my loom up again and this is the first time I've done it since college and I'm stuck, can you please help me? They know they get information so they drive an hour. It's much easier than writing their professors."

"And these people you take down to your studio?"

"Of course, but not someone who wants a show."

"What were some of your considerations about building out here? I mean, if I wanted to have a retail store I wouldn't have come all the way out to the woods to start one."

"It wasn't just for the store," Thurid said, "but also to live here."

"That was part of it . . ." Noel continued, "but, I agree, you wouldn't think you could come out here and make a living. However, we talked to a guy in Florida, New York—and who has ever heard of Florida, New York, right?—and he had a similar set-up. He had moved out to an area where people from New York City had farms, weekend places. He assured us we could make a living away from the city. And this seemed like a logical place. And it is cheaper out here! We don't have to produce or turn the volume that we'd have to do in the city. We own the building so we have no payments to worry about. And life is just cheaper here."

"What were some things you had to give up?"

"Well, the money sort of started quitting me before I quit it. We had a large house in Potomac and we had monthly living expenses that ran to a total of $1,300. That was just so we could stay even! Our house payments with taxes ran close to $500. At the time—two years ago—money was tight and business for the small builder like myself was just dead in the Washington area.

"We had hoped to make a lot of money in the building business and just retire, but that didn't work out. All we had was the equity of the house which was a fair amount of money. When we sold it we had enough money to buy the land, build the shop/studio, stock the shop and live off it for a year and a half.

"Crafts are no different from any business in terms of how

long it takes to get established. Craftsmen now are working for a living; it's not hobbies, and they don't want to put pieces in shops on consignment."

"Did the fact that you had been in business yourself and had those skills, did that make the transition a lot easier for you?"

"I'm not sure about skills," Thurid began, "but we had the right attitude. We never had a steady income in the building business. We were either real rich or real broke. We weren't used to having security. Our friends, suburban friends, couldn't understand why I didn't shoot myself."

"Were there any problems within the community here?" we asked.

They shook their heads.

"Do they come up to see your stuff?"

They shook their heads, laughed.

Thurid said, "We're the hippies on the hill."

"I do think that more and more people know what we're doing, but they don't understand why people would pay the prices we're asking," Noel said.

The door of the shop opened and we could hear voices, Thurid went out to see who had come in and we asked Noel what sort of crafts background he had had.

"Well, I saw someone making a pot and went out and bought a potter's wheel . . . simple as that . . . but I tried it and found out it didn't work. This was years ago. Then Thurid met a woman who was a potter and was interested in learning how to weave so Thurid taught her to weave and this woman taught me to make pots.

"From then on I've worked on my own, taken short courses and since I've been out here I have had the opportunity to have a production potter here and work with him, side by side."

"Where are you in your development as a craftsman? Do you plan to take more courses?"

"No, I don't think so, not in the sense of going to a college and taking classes. Most of the courses are geared for people who aren't as far along as I am. I do go to lectures and workshops by famous potters. I attend them all. It's not technical problems that I have, but inspiration, stimulation."

"The chance to share ideas?"

"Yes, and now I'm teaching at a local community college. That helps. It helps my own development."

"You learn from that process?"

"Sure."

"How much time do you spend in actual production?"

"I guess my work breaks down something like this. Mondays are off. We decided that we need a break, a chance to get away from it. So we go into Washington, visit shows, see people. I then spend Tuesday, Wednesday and Friday actually producing."

"Are these eight-hour days?"

"More like twelve-hour days. I get to the studio by eight in the morning and quite often I'm here until ten at night."

"How much of that time is actually at the wheel?"

"Oh, only a fourth of the time . . . there are kilns to fire, mixing . . . that sort of thing. Thursdays I teach, but I work in the morning, though I don't throw. I clean up, put hands on pieces I made Wednesday.

"On weekends I come over early, do restocking, but I spend my time in the shop. I do some silversmithing just to keep busy when there's no one around. Thurid doesn't like keeping shop so I usually do it."

"Are you at the point now where you can make a living off this?"

"Yeah . . . our needs and wants are simple. If we were living in the city it wouldn't be enough, but here in the country it's comfortable."

"What advice would you give a couple like yourselves that were trying to make the transition . . . trying to run a shop/ studio full time?"

"There are several things you have to consider initially. For example, if you're going to open a retail store in a city or an area with a high street traffic then the chances of doing this and being a production craftsman are slim. You've got to make up your mind whether you're going to produce or run a shop. I think if you're in a rural area where traffic is down and you know when you're going to have traffic through the shop then you can handle it. I know potters who only open up on weekends.

"It's also one thing to be selling your own thing, another to be selling other work. I think you owe it to your craftsmen to be open and expose their crafts to the public. So anyone going into the crafts business has to decide what they want to produce, and a lot of people don't know that.

"You take away your normal income and make woodworking, pottery or weaving a profession and its an entirely different thing, because in order to survive you have to make some production pieces, repeated pieces, and a lot of people don't like that.

"Also, you should be well capitalized. You should be able to survive at least a year without touching any money from the sales. A year is minimum. And if you're going to sell other crafts it's important to know some of the processes that go into the work. It also takes time to find the work of other craftsmen. I'd say to develop the list of people you want and can count on takes about two years."

"How many different craftsmen do you have?"

"About forty."

"How do you decide whom to take? Are they just famous? Or are they local?"

"We sell only pieces that we like. You have to watch out so you don't take pieces you know you can sell, but that you don't like. It's tempting, but in the long run that can hurt you."

"Do you make certain decisions about price ranges? Is it cheaper to buy a pot here than in the city?"

"Our prices are the same as the city, but we're not carrying the same pots, of course, that you'd find in Washington. Our range is in pots, well, forty dollars is the highest price. We tend toward functional pots; we don't have funky ceramics."

"How do you feel putting up your pots for sale?"

"Well, we have thirteen potters' work here and I really like it when someone picks my pot out of all of them and says, 'Gee, isn't this a great pot!' But it's terrible when they walk through the door and say, 'We've heard about you . . . what pots are yours?' You know they're not going to like them."

"To go back to prices, was there a decision to keep them low?"

"I feel this way: if I'm not willing to pay so much for a pot and can't justify a retail price, then I don't buy it for the shop."

"Have you done any work on cost efficiency, volume?"

"You know, all those marketing terms . . . I just don't know them. We total up the weekend sales and monthly totals, compare those, and we run non-scientific studies about what place in the shop sells better."

"Is display important?"

"Very. But if you have a well-crafted piece it will eventually appeal to someone. One thing I have learned in marketing, if you have a piece you're ashamed of, you tend to put it back in a corner, hide it. The thing to do is place it out on the counter where everyone can see it, but then you have to look at it all the time."

"How do people hear about you?"

"Word of mouth. Being out and away from the city, people like to discover you and then they like to bring their friends back, show them what they've found. We haven't done any publicizing except for one flyer when we opened. Some newspapers have done us up because we're a bit unusual."

"Do you think the arrangement now with the craftsman getting fifty percent of the retail price about right? You're both of the people in this issue: craftsman and retailer!"

"On certain items . . . pottery, jewelry, yes, but not weaving or wood. It's never been that way for them. But for people who open a shop and think they can do it on a twenty-five percent mark up, they just can't. There is not a high enough volume in the craft business.

"Now some craftsmen think they can keep the price low by selling themselves at fairs, etc. But they're forgetting the time involved in selling their own work. Time that takes them away from production."

"Did you consider any other business relating to crafts before you made this move?"

"Yeah, we could have opened a crafts shop in the city, then I thought of providing work space and equipment for craftsmen. I know that's a good business . . . but it's a business.

"When I was selling houses I used to receive a piece of paper in the mail for twenty-five thousand or so, a big wad of money at once, but here at Tollhouse the first few days we'd have twenty dollars in real cash and it was a much better feeling than getting those checks in the mail."

"Are you working harder now than when you were building?"

"I'm working harder, making less money and enjoying it more."

"Were you working nine-to-five before?"

"Oh, no, not that much. I was rather lazy. But the kind of work I did before was often business on the phone, in the evening . . . shouting at subcontractors about getting a job done."

"Were you a carpenter?"

"No, I had a crew. I'd bang nails, or bend nails as they'd say, with them."

"What is your background?"

"Photography actually. My father was a photographer. I grew up in the business, and in carpentry. My grandfather was a carpenter. But I made my living as a freelance photographer with Black Star."

"Why did you leave photography?"

"I was doing fine, at the top of the business, and decided to build a house. I loved that, outdoors, working with my hands, being away from the pressures of the telephone."

"Do you do any photography now?"

"No, I'm a rank amateur."

"Then you could say there was some sort of creativity that you needed and you moved through photography, carpentry, now pottery. But do you get more satisfaction out of pottery or are we going to come back in two years and find you raising horses?"

"No. You'll find me downstairs making pots. The other

activities didn't have the texture that I needed to make me satisfied."

The customers left and Thurid returned to the lounge, saying, "I hate to take people's money. Just now they left it on the counter and I almost wrapped it in the package. I enjoy talking to people, but then taking their money still troubles me."

"How long, Thurid, have you been working as a weaver?"

"Over ten years."

"You work on the loom?"

"Yes, but it doesn't look it. I do a lot of hand finishing."

"You make functional pieces?"

"Only one piece, which is my production piece."

"Thurid," volunteered Noel, "is the better craftsman. She has the better reputation. Internationally known!"

"Whatever that means!" Thurid laughed.

Thurid has had shows in Norway and pictures of her work in *Craft Horizons*.

"I've worked hard on getting a reputation," Thurid continued, "so before I started selling I went to all the shows. I really worked hard."

"How do you relate to each other's work?"

"Well, we're very critical of each other," Noel said. "If Thurid doesn't like a piece of mine, she'll tell me."

"I'm afraid I'm very outspoken, a lot cruder. Noel's very nice. He generally doesn't like my colors. Sometimes I won't like a pot, some I like very much. But we really have much of the same taste, don't we?" She glanced at Noel who nodded. "That's why it's easy to buy for the shop."

"Isn't that necessary? To have a certain tone or mood for your shop?" we asked.

"Yes, I think that's true. That's why they come out here," Thurid answered. "People walk into the shop and they know they're walking into some personal judgment. And we've made that known. We only have pieces that we like. And we like crude pieces. I love primitive art, for example. I think it's neat to have things that you personally like and if people don't like it they can go elsewhere."

"How much do you do with the business, Thurid?"

"Oh, very little. Noel does it all."

"Thurid writes the letters."

"Do you both do the displays?"

"We did, but I got tired of that so now Noel does most."

"How much time, Thurid, do you spend on your craft?"

"Well, the children leave at eight o'clock. I get over here after the dishes and cleaning up, by nine certainly. Then I work straight until three-thirty when the children come home on the bus."

"Who's idea was it to go full time in crafts?"

"Mine." Thurid smiled. "I had been unhappy as a prosperous builder's wife for a long time and I just didn't like the people we were involved with."

"You don't convey that—you seem very open to people."

"Well, I'm not interested in people people, suburban types."

"Do you find that working in crafts relieves a lot of tension? Is it very satisfying?"

"Tremendously."

"Making a nice pot is more satisfying than building a new house," Noel said.

"We enjoy just really simple, simple things now. Like opening Noel's kiln this afternoon, that's a family affair. We all join in. It's neat."

"But, of course," added Noel, "we had the other things first. I had an airplane, a sports car, all the toys. We had everything but it didn't make us happy. We got trapped in bills."

"Everything was very materialistic," Thurid continued. "We had money and other people were impressed. It was really horrible."

"Do you find that you have more time now to work on your crafts? More time than before?"

"Oh, yes! And it's a big transition from being a rich suburban housewife who weaves . . . that just didn't seem right. It didn't fit. Now I consider myself a craftsman and that's a profession. And it's a whole lot better for our relationship, Noel and I; I feel more fulfilled, valuable."

"I think we both feel this. Our lives are more valuable, have more meaning and make more sense."

BILL COOK

Metalsmith Bill Cook has two studios in Washington, one at the Watergate and one in Georgetown, both with Chelsea Court. Chelsea Court, the creation of Maxine Brown, consists of retail stores with working craftsmen on display in open studios.

Bill is a known figure in the Washington craft world because several years ago he took a simple design of a metal mobile and made it into a wind chime. It caught on in retail stores around the country and Bill has an extremely successful business, doing what he likes to do best.

We had talked with Bill several times in doing the preliminary research for this book and we had talked also about how he was able to make a go of it in craft production. He was used to our questions, so when we did the interview at his Watergate studio Bill kept working, polishing metal as he talked.

Bill is in his late twenties but looks like a teenager. In his studio he gives the first impression of just playing around with scraps of metal, but there is little wasted motion and a certain sureness with his hand. If he hadn't become a craftsman he might have gone into medicine, a surgeon.

"Bill, one thing you mentioned before was the value of design. You started with one wind chime, a solid design, and then were able to broaden that out, make adjustments."

"Actually it all started with scraps of metal that I had hanging around the place and I decided I was going to string them up into a mobile because I didn't want to waste them. There was no real attempt to design at that point. It was just a bunch of scraps and it was just going to be a funky thing, very folkish.

"When I assembled the scraps of metal I found out I had sound. Not a good sound. But it indicated that sound was another possibility for a mobile. So from that point I started the sophistication of both these elements, the design quality of the thing and the sound quality, and then the integration of the elements: sound, form, movement, color. Now it's at the point where I'm running at a pretty high level of sophistication of these things."

"How many different designs have you worked out?"

"Oh, I'd say pretty close to thirty, both designs and variations."

"What enabled you to take this one design or notion that came along by accident and make it work? Was this some knowledge you had from school?"

"Absolutely not! In fact, at that point I hadn't even learned how to handle a welding torch. It was just sort of a natural interest. It sparked the mind. You know you start out very naively from a general concept to focusing more and more on the details. It happened for me to be very natural. After a certain point I began to be aware of what I was doing, but not for quite a while . . ."

"What was the immediate craft for you before metal? Were you in metal?"

"Ah . . . the first craft I did was enamel. And the next I experienced was clay; after that came metal."

"You mentioned earlier that you thought design was very important for a crafts person . . ."

"Without a doubt. I had had a course and had all this design training. My assembling the first little wind chime all happened after four and a half years of school. So I had design theory which I used automatically."

"When you discovered your wind chimes and were able to do them one at a time, what were the steps that you took so you could make a living out of them?"

"The first time I began to sell these in great number was at the American Craft Council Northeast Craft Fair. I would venture to say this particular fair has set up more craftsmen in business than anything else I know of. I went up there about four years ago."

"Where were you working then?"

"I was working with a store, a craft retail store that I helped start with a friend of mine. I was running that and working in my studio. That was here in Georgetown, the American Hand.

"Anyway, at the fair I got such a good response from people buying that I decided I could begin to rely on this as a form of income. I got several thousand dollars' worth of orders within a few hours and as time went on I got reorders and that continued to the point where I started to take on apprentices.

"I kept growing like that while at the same time I became more aware of production methods that would allow me to make these chimes more rapidly and have them better crafted."

"After the American Hand you moved into Chelsea Court. What are the advantages of Chelsea Court for you?"

"Well, there're several. One is, the rent is very economical for the space and service that I get . . . I have someone answering my phone calls, someone checking mail. This is all very important when you're in contact with a lot of stores. All this is very handy. But the major attraction is that I can deal with the public and the public's reaction to my work. There's this instant test marketing situation. Also, retail store owners walk into Chelsea Court and ask if I'll wholesale to them. So the exposure is very good for business."

"How big is your wholesale business?"

"I sell to fifty stores."

"Have the apprenticeships worked out?"

"Very well for me. I don't believe the craftsman today can economically continue to produce original designs at a price that most people can afford. So part of his artistic endeavor has to be spent on reproducing some of his designs. And a craftsman has to make some variations on a theme because he doesn't have an endless supply of ideas. Therefore, he has to do some production or turn toward another source of income. Now that doesn't mean a production craftsman makes identical pieces. These pieces have at least subtle variations."

"How many apprentices do you have?"

"About four at a time. I have voluntary apprentices—they work for the experience—and also salaried ones. The problem most craftsmen have with apprentices is that they don't know how to manage and delegate authority to the apprentices."

"How long do they stay with you?"

"It varies. If they want to learn the whole business then it's about a year. Others just like to do one or the other aspect of metal and that's easily taught."

"I see you're still working on the individual pieces."

"I keep saying I'll never tie another knot as long as I live, but I'm still at it . . . I'm going to try to do unique work soon."

"So you're moving into new areas . . . ?"

"Right. Well, I've always wanted to but it's just been a question of time and finances to do it. You know you can become a prisoner of your own work. That happens to a production craftsman. He soon finds that if he has produced something that has a market he ends up not having enough time to do new and innovative work.

"It's very difficult for a craftsman to stop and develop something new when it's going to cost him thirty dollars or so a day that he could be earning by filling an order. It requires discipline. And a certain amount of security. Plus there's no point—artistically—to continue doing the same thing over and over."

"But will you stay in metal?"

"Not necessarily. I just happened to have a facility in it; I like it. But I have had extensive training in pottery, sculpture. I have also carved stone and I've worked in wood. And I've also worked in jewelry and silver. I prefer to think of myself as a designer who will execute an idea in the media that would give it the best result."

"You've mentioned before that there were certain crafts like weaving that didn't lend themselves to production."

"Yes, that's unfortunately true. Weaving is such an intensive thing. Keeping a loom threaded properly, the time it takes to do a simple piece. It's difficult for a craftsman to compete with the machine. The fabric designers are in the same problem. They can't compete against mass-produced items.

"What happens is the manufacturer will get a good artist who will design an original piece and get paid two thousand or so, which is fine, and then the manufacturer will reproduce the piece by the hundreds and thousands of yards."

"If someone wanted to repeat your experience, set himself up as a craftsman, what would it cost him for a studio?"

"My studio is not typical. It doesn't fall into a particular craft. I work in metal, plastic, enameling, jewelry. I have about a thousand dollars of equipment here and at the other studio. In my work I work simply."

"Well, with that little invested, can you make a living? Others have mentioned to me that they expect to make about twenty thousand a year from their craft. Is that unrealistic?"

"No. I heard of a potter up in the Northeast who is grossing over sixty thousand a year in retail sales. It means he's making about twenty-five thousand, but he's producing. Now I still need the help of apprentices to make a living. I should think that a person who has a good quality product, well-designed, and who behaves in a businesslike manner and persists can make it."

"What are some of the commonsense things you have learned in setting up this business?"

"One of the first things is to understand that the stores the craftsmen are dealing with aren't taking advantage of them. The craftsman has to understand that he had to make the item profitable to the store owner. A craftsman needs the store to survive, so he has to understand the needs of the owner. A craftsman has to keep that in mind all the time."

"And much depends on how much an item is priced at?"

"Yes. I try to decide how much I should price an item in terms of the retail price. You have to know what people are paying, and today that's somewhere between ten and twenty dollars. A little higher in jewelry. That's the price range where I focus most of my stuff. The next bracket is under fifty dollars.

"So I suggest that the crafts person find out what the general range of prices is at the particular store. Another thing I always do is agree to exchange items that have been purchased from me. These are the higher priced items. Therefore, the store owner isn't stuck with an expensive work. This also allows me to raise the percentage on expensive items I have on display in stores around the country.

"A craftsman has to give. He has to realize how much of a

chance a store is taking because the retail business is so unpredictable. Another way I try to help stores is to put together a package deal for new stores that are taking my work on for the first time. This usually is on a consignment basis."

"Do you do your own bookkeeping, all of that work?"

"I have, but this year I'm getting an accountant. Actually what I do now is train one of the apprentices to do it. Just minor bookkeeping. I'd like to get to the point in the business where I don't know what is going on. Just keep check on the quality, that's all."

"What are your long-range plans?"

"Oh, set up a design firm, a situation that's sort of happening here now in a miniature sort of way. I would like to be able to do one-of-a-kind pieces as well as design for industry, anything from birdbaths to tea cups, in all media. And have a small production area."

"One thing we haven't covered, Bill, is your school history."

"Well, I started in California at Claremont Men's College majoring in business, but I flunked economics and got a D in accounting so I had to change majors quickly. I then majored in art which at the time was only a minor for me. I took my first art course at the Scripps College which was on the same campus. Then I took a course in design and got absolutely enraptured by it. It became apparent that I should go to art school so I transferred to Otis Art Institute in Los Angeles. At the time I was involved in clay, but also going through a disciplined curriculum of fine arts. This was dry and difficult, but was important to know. After two years I wanted to do just pottery and so I came back East to set myself up as a potter.

"I arrived in D.C. and found that materials were expensive; I couldn't afford a gas kiln and I just became defeated by the mechanics of the situation. I then ended up messing around with enamel and copper . . . what I had done in that design course nearly four years before. I got a torch and taught myself how to use it and this is how I got into metal work."

"So that was all self-education?"

"Yes. I didn't really do very much metal work while in art school."

"What should a student do in the way of education?"

"Well, somehow get a good design background. Go to some ordinary department that has a good design program. And at the same time as he or she is learning design, they can pick up the craft media. Study two- and three-dimensional design; here in Washington some of the best drawing and painting courses are at the Smithsonian Associates program, not very expensive. In design courses you learn the way to see shapes. It's a tremendous asset.

"One of the common beliefs is that you can apprentice yourself to someone and learn all there is to know. I don't think so. You take people getting into leather . . . they buy a few tools, work with someone for a while making belts and next thing they're calling themselves leathersmiths; well, that's hardly true.

"Anyone can be a technician. The difficult part comes in how well the person conceives an idea, how innovative the work is. What new ideas will be added to the body of knowledge about the craft? Much of this comes from formal education. You can learn many things as an apprentice, but you can't learn all. You need that formal education, that design education."

"How do you design?"

"I do a lot of it in my head. I look at a shape and wonder . . . I am a person who works directly, a media person working in objects themselves."

"Do you try to make a statement with your work?"

"In the last few years I have become a creature of motion. I love to sail, I love to dance, I love to move. These things all work with the wind. Graceful movement, simple movement. It's harmonious movement. I would say simply about my work that I'm very interested in working with the free and natural elements of nature. The older I get the more things I can eliminate from my work.

"I want to work with my hands and my eyes. I'm a visually oriented person. And once a person gets turned on to working with their hands, seeing the object created, then they're never satisfied doing anything else. I don't know whether that means making a statement or not, but it's what makes me happy."

SOLVEIG COX

Solveig Cox is a potter who works out of her home in Hollin Hills, a section of Alexandria, Virginia, just across the Potomac from Washington, D.C., and on the way toward Mount Vernon. Her house is on a small hill overlooking the cul-de-sac of the neighborhood, and the ground floor is given over to her wheels, shelves of work, benches and tables. However, she does share her studio with a washer and dryer and the telephone. The telephone she keeps close because she likes to talk on the phone while she works.

Solveig Cox is well-known in Washington and across the country for her small, indoor water fountains. They come in a variety of sizes, but always a woman and a small daughter holding jugs that spill water into a ceramic bowl. She has been making these fountains for nearly eight years and they are the mainstay of her production pieces. She also makes a series of what she calls "little people" and lately, influenced by a trip to Turkey and Greece, small ceramic dolls.

We talked while Solveig did some hand building on a fountain, working at a bench in the front of the studio near the expanse of windows. Solveig is a strong, healthy, attractive woman who doesn't seem old enough to have a son twenty and a daughter eighteen. She is quick to smile and although serious about her craft she doesn't take herself seriously. She is ready to laugh about her success and ready to share what she knows about pottery and how to make a living working in ceramics. We asked how she got into pottery in the first place.

"In college, at Bennington."

"You studied crafts in college?"

"Not exactly. I would have been a graphics major if I had graduated, but I got married instead. Then my husband was in OCS and wives weren't allowed on base and my mother, who was a crafts person herself, Mariska Karasz, an embroiderer and dress designer, told me to go out and do, and I did. I guess I always knew I'd have a career of some kind.

"I continued to study pottery when we were in Germany and after coming back to Washington I set up my own studio. I had two children then, but I could work at home and take care of them. It was perfect."

"When was it that you set up your studio and began production work?"

"That was in 1961. My first pots were terrible. My mother-in-law had given me a hundred dollars to buy our first kiln, an electric one, and my husband built the wheel. The investment really was minimal. I keep telling kids who come to me that it isn't hard to do if you want to do it. It takes work, that's all. I invested two hundred dollars and got that back right away and my income doubled every year and it continued to double, though it isn't doubling these last years."

"How do you sell?"

"Wholesale. Three-quarters of my business is wholesale. A quarter is retail from the house. I think we could do more retail if we didn't live where we do and if I wanted to spend more time developing the retail side. I don't encourage retailing because of living in a residential area."

"How does your day break down? How much time goes into production, packing?"

"Well, I hire someone to pack because that's the worst job and she comes in when I have a shipment ready. On that day I sort out the stuff. Usually I come down to work as close to eight o'clock as possible. I break at one o'clock for lunch and then I work till five or six. I work a five-day week except pre-Christmas when it's every day and far into the night to get orders finished."

"When you began to get into crafts did you see it as an income? It wasn't just a hobby, was it?"

"Oh, no, it was a job. We were hungry then and I think that helped." She said laughing. "For me it's a drive. I know sometimes when I don't have a trip or a college payment or income tax to meet I don't push myself. But when I was starting out we had just bought a new house. We were also just back from Germany and had to cut down our standard of living and that was really painful. I'd think of things that would sell because I found myself spending the money before I made it. Those were the days when you could buy lobsters and if I got a good kilning I'd buy lobsters. I think hunger had a lot to do with my early success."

"Have you developed a series that's your own?"

"Well, I'm really involved with little-people pots. For some reason that is a seller. And my fountains are a big seller. I really make money from my fountains because they retail for a hundred sixty dollars now. And I can't do enough."

"Did you design it?"

"Yes. A landscape architect called me once and asked if I did commissions, and I thought, 'Wow, garden walls, fountains . . . what's he going to ask for?' Well, he came and he wanted a coffee cup for his wife!" She laughed.

"But he started me thinking and that was terrific, though he never did buy a fountain once I started making them. The little people I started doing in Germany. They developed out of the handbuilding I had been doing there. It's a form of amusement creating these little people; they're fun."

"Do you still handbuild the little people?"

"No, most are wheel turned, but I add on. There are very few pots that go out of here that don't have additions to them. I do very few straight pots because straight pots don't sell.

"I don't spend much time throwing. My throwing is adequate, but I don't get that much kick out of it." She glanced up from her work and added smiling, "No pun intended."

"You like to handbuild?"

"Well, yes, but I guess I really like the results from the bank."

The telephone rang and Solveig took it and kept working. It was a neighbor calling. "I always have work by the phone," she explained hanging up. "I love to talk on the telephone."

"Go back a moment to the difference between handbuilding and throwing. Why do you prefer handbuilding?"

"Because what I do to a pot with a face or hair, that sells it. I really get a big charge out of doing the first ones, but after a while I can sit and talk and I don't even have to think about them. They're easy that way."

"Have you used apprentices?"

"Yes, I have had several girls. I recently had one girl who is now at Alfred University and she came to me as a high school student and just put hair on my sculptures, then she got so she could fire. When she came back recently from Alfred she could throw better than I! That was wonderful to see."

"Do you think a young person today could be a production potter and make a living at it?"

"Damn well can, but they have to work."

"Do they also have to have a sense of design, imagination?"

"Not necessarily. I think you can market anything if you do it right."

"How would you suggest they do it? Go to school? Get a formal education?"

"If they can afford it, a liberal arts education makes them much more of a person than art school does. Too many kids go to art school because they think they don't have to work. Art's easy, they think. That's nonsense! Whatever they are going to make it in takes work."

"Why liberal arts?"

"Because to work by yourself, cut off from people while doing a craft, you need to first have that formal kind of education in literature, history and the like that makes you a well-rounded person. In art schools you don't get that background."

"So you'd suggest a person go to a liberal arts school and then pick up the skills of a craft on the side?"

"Well, I think you either have the skills or you don't."

"What about the business end? Have you had some business training?"

"I've been lucky. My husband does all my taxes for me. But if you don't have someone like a husband to do it, you can always hire a person. It really isn't that difficult. I have had people say to me, 'You were able to start potting because you had a husband to support you, etc.' There's a lot to that. But I also had a husband and children to take care of at the same time. I had my responsibilities to live with. I think a single person can do it, but it's not simple. I just can't say how much work it takes to make a career in crafts."

"What about when you first started selling your pots?"

"Oh, I just filled my basket with goodies and went from place to place. I had to go through the embarrassment of someone saying no. And once at the Artist Mart in Georgetown when I said to them that I couldn't understand why my pots weren't selling, the woman said, 'Well, they're not very good.' That was awful, but it was the kind of challenge I needed."

"How long do you think it takes for a person to become a self-sufficient craftsman?"

"I had a woman who came to me several years ago. I trained her and it took her about three years to make it. She's doing very well now."

"Do you think there are certain things that you could learn at art school, such as design, that are important to your pottery?"

Solveig thought for a while and kept working, then she shook her head. "No, I think most design courses do more harm than good. I don't know why I feel that way." She shook her head. "I guess because I grew up in a family where good design was all-important. Of course, my husband kids me, says, 'And who said you had perfect taste?' " She laughed again.

"Do you consider yourself an artist, a craftsman, a housewife?"

"A potter. I don't make it into the big shows where I would be considered an artist, but I console myself on the way to the bank. My stuff is pretty cute, I guess; it's not intellectual."

"Where's the fun for you in ceramics?"

"I enjoy manipulating clay and the satisfaction also of having all those boxes out there all packed. I have the fantasy of having my own truck saying Cox Pottery . . . but that kind of thing will never happen. Every time I turn something over to someone else it's different. It's not really my work and how many compromises am I willing to make? I think I've made them all. I want to stop now and control my work."

"How do you sell now?"

"I don't take orders. I don't want to fill an order for twelve items. I just want shops to say, 'I've seen what you have.' I have come far enough to be able to afford to say no."

"Do you think of your work as an art object or something utilitarian?"

"Not as an art object. My work is more decorative. I'm not really saying something. I'm not making big statements, at least I'm not conscious of making statements. Some people say my work is whimsical. Perhaps that's true."

"Well, you have a lot of that whimsical quality in your personality. Does that then come out in your pots?"

"Whimsical?" Solveig laughed. "Well I really like doing pottery. I don't see why one has to be deadly serious about the work."

"Do you teach?"

"No. I don't consider myself that good a teacher and I just can't make as much money teaching."

"How do you decide how much your time is worth?"

"I base it on my throwing time. I have to throw thirty dollars' worth of stuff an hour. Then it takes another hour of handbuilding, that brings my rate down to fifteen dollars an hour."

"How do you base your prices on items?"

"Well, for example, I threw eight of these new hanging people-pots in a half hour. Then it took me another hour and a half to finish them. It should take me an additional hour to hang the string and get them ready. And they wholesale for seven-fifty each. I first asked my husband if he thought twenty-five dollars was too much for the traffic to bear. He said that was just right, then I knew I had jacked up the price too much. He's always overpricing."

"Do you go to the fairs?"

"Oh, yes. I plan on going to the Northeast Fair again this year, and selling. I get a big charge out of retailing my stuff, hearing what people say. I got my first big break wholesaling from the Northeast Fair and also from America House. They were the first to market my stuff."

"How did that fountain get onto the market?"

"Well, I took it to New York, to America House. I remember it was just before Christmas and I flew to New York carrying my fountain under my arm. I was thinking I'd ask thirty-five dollars wholesale for it, and was worried it was too much. When I went in to see Mr. Rogers he looked at the fountain and said, 'Oh, this is very nice. This could be a catalog piece next year.' They immediately priced the fountain for a hundred and twenty retail. That meant sixty dollars for me. Now I'm making eighty dollars a fountain. Really, it just doesn't seem possible!"

"How many fountains do you make a year?"

"About two hundred and fifty."

"And it's still fun making them?"

"Oh, yes, especially when I'm on my way to the bank. You know," she added after a moment, "it's very nice being self-sufficient and successful at something, especially at pottery, which everybody thinks of as a hobby and something you do on Saturday mornings." She waved her hand around at her big and crowded studio. "Who needs women's liberation when you have all this?"

RON GOODMAN

Ron Goodman's apartment in northwest Washington is in a grand old building. In another age it would have been stately, but the building has gone to seed like the neighborhood. Lately, however, a group of young craftsmen, and young people in general, have moved back into the area, houses are being remodeled, vacant lots turned into parks. New galleries are opening, and artists are establishing studios.

Ron's apartment—which is also his studio—is vast, with high ceilings and large windows, and empty of furniture. When I visited in the late fall there were only scattered pillows, a second-hand couch. All was shoved into one corner to allow space for a giant blue crocheted "thing," as Ron called it, that hung from the ceiling like soft cobweb.

"That took me four months to finish," Ron explained, leading me through the trappings. "It's a hunderd and ten feet long and has over thirty thousand stitches. The object, which dominates the room, dwarfs Ron. He appeared even slighter and less than his five-seven. The only massive thing about Ron is his blond beard.

But he's not a gentle man. In the long afternoon of talking he displayed a mind that was ordered, disciplined and quick to make pronouncements. His strength shows also in his craft: his variety of fabric constructions all have power, a certain wildness and show of color. They make statements that tell the viewer much about the artist.

Ron Goodman is perhaps the best-known Washington craftsman. Much of his work is now in galleries and museums, and at times pieces circulate through the United States as part of the Museum of Contemporary Crafts show "Sculpture in Fiber."

He began crafts late, in 1961 when he was bored with the army and walked into a crafts center at Fort Ord in California. After that it was an AA in ceramics from Los Angeles City College, a BA in fabrics, design and art history from California State College at Long Beach, then an MFA in fabric from Cranbrook Academy of Art. He followed that up with two consecutive Fulbright scholarships to study the fabric arts and crafts in India.

Ron defines himself as an artist-craftsman and refuses to make a living off his art. "There's no way I can put a value on my work. Even if I were to charge by the hour no one could afford the pieces. Therefore, I make my living teaching and lecturing. I don't depend on my work for an income. In fact, financially these sculptures are a loss, materials alone are incredibly expensive. Even if I were only to charge five cents an hour who's going to pay for something that took me four months to complete?"

While he talked Ron spoke with his hands. They continually moved, summed up situations with a twist, backed off a question, found another answer with a roll of both hands. He also talked with his huge hundred-and-ten-foot art in view—not that it was easy to avoid the dangling crochet—as if gaining ideas from his creation.

"I started by trying to make my hobby, which it was, my vocation. What a beautiful way to exist, I thought. I worked hard at this, harder than most. I still do work hard. I also have worked in industry and I have taught.

"I was at one university where they wanted me to stay, give me tenure. But I won't do it. It becomes too easy to relax, get satisfied. I force myself to stay on my toes.

"It's incredibly difficult to make money out of what you do in crafts. That is, to be an artist and make one-of-a-kind pieces. You might have a craftsman home from college with a degree, for example, being supported by parents for a few years while he's down in the basement throwing pots.

"Then a local store owner telephones him, says he heard the crafts person has a degree in art, and wants him to come down and do a window display. The crafts person will make some money, fine, and the store owner will be pleased, ask for another window to be done and then there will be more and more . . . so now what is the potter? A window dresser!"

Ron has been speaking slowly, carefully, perched on the edge of the secondhand couch, eager for the questions, eager to reply, but selecting the words, deciding on the choices like pieces of fabric. His voice is soft, not much metal to it, but the resolutions of his convictions carry weight and authority. We found we didn't want to doubt him: he had fought all these battles.

"If you look at my graduate school, Cranbrook, which is one of the top five places for crafts, each year they graduate about seventy-five students. Perhaps one or two will make it as an artist. And they're the very best! The best training, best equipment, the latest techniques. If this class can't make it as artists, who can? The socioeconomics of the United States are against them."

"Then what do you tell a young crafts person who wants a career as an artist?"

"I'd advise the person who wants to do crafts as an art form to have some sort of basic income. Something that's least offensive to the person. Driving a taxi, whatever. Just so the rest of the time will be free to work on crafts."

We wanted to know how it was that he could be successful as an artist-craftsman when so many others had failed. The question was longer than that and rambling, tangential. He was ready with his reply, anxious to answer before we could finish. He cut corners on the question to get his answer stated.

"I've been lucky. It's like starting a business. For every ten businesses that open a year only one or two make it. What that says to me is that if anyone wants to make a success of something it can't be part-time. It can't be something you go to as a job. If you really want to make a success of it first you have to be dedicated and be willing to make sacrifices. Then you're not going to get the financial success that doing something else might bring you . . . but you'll be happier.

"There are not many people at this point who are willing to do this, but there will be more. I see a lot of young people who want to achieve this lifestyle, if you want to call it that. But they haven't confronted the realities of the socioeconomics of this society.

"They are generally quite young and haven't had many life experiences. They'll say, 'Gee, this is great! I want to be an artist!' I sit back and don't tell them a thing; if it works, it works. These young people, however, haven't confronted, aren't even aware of the problems. It will hit them, as it hit me, and that will knock most of them out.

"I'm not out to make my students artists. That's impossible. I tell my students that I'm not teaching art; I'm teaching creativity. Creativity can be taught through any medium. It can be taught through cooking, a job; I happen to teach it through fabrics. To me the joy of my teaching is to have a student come up and say, 'Look what I've done. I've never drawn before and now I can make beauty.' That's a very rewarding result."

"Do people change lifestyles after they get into crafts? Do you see much of this?"

Ron shook his head. "Making the decision just to take a crafts course is a pretty big decision. But anyway people don't have to change their lives to be enriched. Most of my classes are women, housewives, and I've noticed that many get turned on to what they are creating and begin to demand more. They refuse to stay home and baby-sit. New arrangements have to be made with the husband because of these craft classes. That's a good sign."

"What if a student came to you and said, 'I want to get seriously into crafts. What would you tell her?"

"I'd tell her not to stay with me, to leave Washington. There's no place around here where a person can get a solid background, for example, in fabrics. I'd send him or her to a school where the history of fabrics is taught, weaving is taught—it takes about ten years to become a good weaver—where the person could get two solid years of dye work, two years of design. With the broad foundation a person is better off because later he or she can build on one aspect of that foundation. I would also advise going to two or more schools, seeking out the fine departments.

"I first majored in ceramics, then I did painting, then weaving, lacemaking, knitting, macramé. I'm into crocheting now. That's what gives me the most enjoyment. An artist wants to know it all. But there's a problem here. It takes about ten years before you're ready to make a statement in a particular form. When an artist jumps around he waters down his statement."

"One last question: Why are so many people becoming interested in crafts?"

"That's simple. They have been dehumanized. Their lives are ordered from nine to five; they have no sense of creativity. They get the feeling: if I wasn't in the office, so what? if I didn't live, so what? Making something, something as simple as knotting, gives a person meaning. It's his statement to the world." Ron waved toward his enormous hanging blue cobweb, "That's my statement. That's the meaning of my last four months." He smiled, proud of his statement and his answer.

PENLAND CRAFTS SCHOOL

They leave the lights on all night at Penland School of Crafts. They light up the huge three stories of Loom House, the pottery workshop, the forge and glassblowing sheds. The lights are left burning because students work late on their crafts, long after sunset, and sometimes—when a kiln is being opened or the forge is operating—into the daylight itself.

Regardless of what hour one approaches the School of Crafts, coming up from Spruce Pine, through the town of Penland itself —now only a post office, a zip code, and railway depot—coming up another few miles, following the curves through forests of North Carolina pines, one can always see the school, bright in the distance. It's pinned into a corner, at the very end of a long sweeping valley and flush against a place called Art'ur's Knob. At night the glow of flames from the forges, the glass shed and the kilns seems to set the base of the Knob on fire.

During the day the setting is not so startling—though it's in view of the long blue ridge of the Black Mountain Range and closer to home, the smooth, green and symmetrical Baileys Peak —as it is tranquil. Here, one thinks, is an isolated corner safe from the abuses of mechanization, the rush of business realities. Within minutes, strangers pick up the easy cadence of the place, the relaxed and friendly atmosphere, the warmth.

According to Bill Brown, director of Penland, nothing is scheduled but meals; and they are kept on time to the minute. The rest of the day falls into place: classes, lectures, free time. People work the way they want. Nothing is planned and everyone finds his or her pace. People "disappear" into their craft, work in solitude at the potter's wheel, or loom, in silence blowing glass. Conversation becomes something of a waste of time. It's not surprising to find a room of thirty potters silently bent over their turning wheels and not a sound, except perhaps the slap of hands against wet clay.

At meals, however, there's a full house of talk and laughter. The dining room, in a grand old stone-and-wood building, with dormitory rooms on top, and a screened-in porch, fills up with 100 students plus 30 faculty and staff. The dining room has the atmosphere of a kibbutz, that closeness of shared lives. Everyone helps with the meals, keeps the place clean.

The food is plentiful and homecooked: brown bread, jams and jellies, biscuits, pancakes for breakfast, ham and thick gravy, then fresh pies and cakes, coffee. Jane Brown, Bill's wife, oversees the kitchen, plans the menus, keeping them varied with tips and suggestions from just about everybody.

Bill Brown makes it to all the meals, though lately he's been avoiding breakfast. "Too many problems in the morning to handle before a cup of coffee. I find if I wait till noon the problems have a way of disappearing."

Brown has been at Penland since 1962, taking over from Miss Lucy Morgan who founded Penland in 1929, a small crafts school that grew out of Miss Lucy's work with the "cottage industry" of weaving and vegetable dyeing in the Appalachian hills. The school grew from a single log cabin and a handful of mountain women into an internationally known craft school that is one of the largest of its kind anywhere. Students have come to Penland from every state and over sixty foreign countries. The crafts taught are ceramics, weaving, glass blowing, graphics, photography, woodworking, vegetable dyeing, lapidary, plastics, jewelry, enameling and sculpture.

"Penland has the finest faculty of any institution of its type," said Bill Brown. "No other school could afford the salaries of the 350 faculty members we have had here during the last eleven years. We can't afford it either, so we don't pay them. They come for room and board, traveling expenses, plus thirty dollars a week spending money. This year alone we're going to have here in ceramics Don Rietz, Toshiko Takaezu, Bill Barrell and Paulus Berensohn, plus Cynthia Bringle; she and Jane Peiser are our resident potters.

"Have you seen the school?" Bill asked. "Come along, I'll show you around."

Bill moves quickly around his school—some 360 acres of mountain land and over forty buildings—at least twice a day he stops by each workshop, has a cup of coffee, a cigarette, and talks to the students. He is over six feet, lanky, has some of the northwest North Carolina tawniness about him. When not in motion, he keeps his sunglasses pushed up on his forehead and unguards his eyes; they bulge, are watery gray and shine as if polished. His hair is thick and long and starting to gray. At first glance, he appears to be a bit seedy: open shirt, old pants, old shoes. Perhaps a history of too many cups of coffee, too many packs of cigarettes. Walking around campus, he is as undistinguished as a student.

"We have six sessions during the summer," he explains, leading me toward his jeep which he parks at random behind the Loom House (there is only one reserved parking spot at Penland; it belongs to Bonnie Ford, the registrar, who has been at the school since 1931). "Last year we had about five hundred fifty students enrolled in twelve courses. We can now house, feed, and provide studio space for one hundred each session. And we take anyone, as long as you're at least eighteen. We have had art students, grandmothers, doctors, lawyers, teachers—and they come in all colors—anyone who wants to learn a craft. Besides the summer courses, we have an eight-week Concentration in the fall and spring. Our expenses every year run close to $325,000, and tuition only pays a third of that. The school has no endowment, so there have been some pretty lean times."

We reached the jeep and drove down the road a quarter-mile to the resident studios where the fellowship craftsmen work. Brown raced the jeep, the only person who ever hurries at Penland, and talked as he drove. "When I first came here, classes had dwindled. Miss Lucy's generation had grown old with her.

"I began by loosening up the place, adding craft courses.

Pretty soon we had a shift in students applying to Penland. Now we're getting a lot more college-age kids. Lots of them are coming two and three years straight. Part of the reason for this is the new interest young people have in crafts. They've heard about Penland—usually from their grandparents who had been students here; we've jumped a generation! Or they have heard about it from craft teachers who might have taught here."

Paulus Berensohn—whose book *Finding One's Way With Clay* had become an overnight bestseller—was teaching that summer session at Penland. When asked why so many outstanding craftsmen come to teach at Penland, he said, "Because of Bill Brown. He's one of the few people anywhere who treats craftsmen as important. He cares about all of us. So we come to teach for him. It would cost Penland about eighty thousand a year if salaries were paid teachers, but we don't want the money. It's a real joy to come up into these hills and be surrounded by other craftsmen and students who love clay, fabrics, wood, and want to make something beautiful from raw materials."

"The only problem," Bill Brown had explained, "is we can't take everyone who applies, either teachers or students. We mail out the applications for summer at the same time, March first, and within five weeks all sessions are full. That's because of the high quality of instruction. We've got Sam Maloof teaching woodwork, Mark Peiser in glass, Gary Noffke in jewelry, Mae Amsler in tapestry; the list goes on like that."

Bill does not teach himself, but he could. He has a BFA and MFA in design from Cranbrook Academy of Art, one of the leading craft schools in America. He had taught design at the University of Delaware, State University of New York at Oswego, Haystack Mountain School of Crafts and at the Worcester Craft Center and Art Museum School, where he was before going to Penland.

Inside the resident studios—a long, two-story building, built plainly of unfinished wood, the exterior being left to age with the seasons—Cynthia Bringle was already at work, putting handles on a row of pots she had just thrown. Along with two others, she was getting a batch of pottery ready for a salt firing.

Cynthia and her sister, Edwina, who is a designer-weaver and has one of the upstairs studios (a long, steeple-ceilinged room filled with five enormous looms, bookcases of fabrics, trunks of woven goods), have been at Penland the longest of the residents, Cynthia coming first as an instructor from Memphis, Tennessee, in the early 1960s. Edwina followed, and now she spends part of her time teaching at colleges.

Most of the waking hours of the residents are spent at their studios. Cynthia averages twelve hours a day working at her craft. "There's no way of making it otherwise: pottery is just that demanding." When not at Penland working or teaching, Cynthia and the other residents are giving shows, demonstration lectures, teaching at craft schools. "Once you're associated with Penland," explained Cynthia, "you can go just about anywhere."

Cynthia and Edwina are what one might call homespun women. They are hardy women, strongly built, but with soft southern voices, gentle ways. Between them and among the other craftsmen, there's the closeness of an extended family, the sharing of ideas, materials, information. Though not on the payroll of Penland—in fact, they pay for studio space—they are ready to help Bill Brown whenever they can, give special lectures each session and are part of the community of Penland, eat their meals in the common dining room with the students.

Cynthia kept working while she visited with us, handling the clay with ease, a minimum of effort; a skill long before perfected. The question this morning that was concerning the craftsmen was about outlets for glasswork. They shared their experiences with galleries and shops, reliability of certain dealers. Among these professionals there's less talk of artistic purposes, theories and techniques, and more concern with shows, wholesaling and retailing, the rising costs of materials and equipment. Hardworking production craftsmen only earn between $7,000 and $12,000, and these are craftsmen at the top of their fields.

Bill Brown has designated positions for all the craftsmen at Penland. They may be fellows or residents, special lecturers or visiting scholars; none of the craftsmen care what they are called. It's enough for them just to be part of Penland.

"Bill's a dictator," Cynthia said, smiling at Bill and explaining why Penland operated so successfully. "He just goes ahead and gets things done."

"The structure and content of the classes, however," Bill added, "is left up to the instructor. Teachers do their own thing, students don't run the classes."

Penland has never experienced any of the struggles and conflicts between students and administrators. The school is totally apolitical. Nowhere on campus is there the familiar graffiti common to college bulletin boards. There has never been a demonstration, sit-in, or drug bust. Most of the reason for this is that students come for short and intense periods of time. Then, too, as Brown says, "The material of crafts keeps a person working. You can't fake it with clay. Political ideology or bullshit doesn't help you make a pot."

While Penland students do visit the resident studios, they usually are too busy themselves to find time. Up at the main Loom House—which shares space with the gift shop, reception, registrar's office, metal workshop, plus Brown's office (which is really only a desk in the storage room) —weaving classes were in session on the second floor, a beautifully large, well-lit, high-ceilinged room that stretches the length and width of the huge building. The Loom House was the second major building Miss Lucy Morgan built at Penland, the gift of Lily Mills in 1944. Before that, Miss Lucy and Penland made do with a collection of small "Lincoln-log" mountain cabins. Her first major building was the original Crafts House, built with donated logs and labor in 1930. Now used as the main dormitory, the Craft House is nicknamed "the giant Lincoln-log set."

Classes at Penland are not formal. Instructors move from person to person, teach individually. "Learning," according to Bill Brown, "is the most natural thing for man to do. We have just made it unnatural. No one has to *learn* here. We don't in that sense *teach* anyone. We just do the best job we can while they're here, but I'm not sure what that really is."

While classes are in session, music plays in the background. The craftsmen vary in musical taste. Weavers tend toward classical music, the metalsmiths play albums of folk, and the potters turn on cassettes of hard rock. Downstairs, the band saws and electric equipment of the woodworkers stop any attempt at music, and those working in the forge and glassblowing sheds are too involved to care about sound.

The glassblowers work two at a time on four-hour shifts that stretch around the clock. They keep busy moving back and forth between the open slit in the furnace and their work stations. They are intense with their jobs, serious behind smoked glasses. A student may work a long shift without speaking a word. It is not a craft that they can be casual about. The molten glass glowing at the end of a length of pipe is dangerous and red as a sore. And delicate. It shapes itself with just a breath of air.

Several years ago, one of the dancers that Bill Brown invited to the school as a visiting scholar choreographed the movements of the glassblowers into a dance and performed it at the school. Bill Brown invites dancers, poets, actors to the school, not to teach, but to be available to students for discussions and special lectures. "Art and history and literature," says Bill Brown, "all tie together. Education is too segmented; we try and bring the subjects together without making a big point of it. I try doing things like this so it doesn't seem all planned. Life around here is the best when I work indirect."

Not all the students who come to study at Penland want to be craftsmen. Early one morning—well before six o'clock—a young woman was already at work in the Loom House, hand-weaving on one of the four-harness looms. Her husband was a glassblower and working the early morning shift; she had gotten up with him to weave. He was a computer programmer, and she was in her second year of law school. Both were spending their vacations at the school.

"We just like the atmosphere," she explained, gazing out at the valley that approaches the school. "It's idyllic and unreal and has nothing to do with what's happening out there, but it's wonderful for a while, and we're just thankful such a place exists."

Students here for only a short summer session become possessive about the place within a few weeks and, if they stay for a second term, resentful of new students, strangers.

"We hold a party the night before the end of each session,"

Bill explained. "An auction party. It ends up being a catharsis for the group. The faculty does the auctioneering and we sell anything. Edwina, for instance, will make some brown bread, or someone will sell a warm can of beer. And, of course, fine pieces of individual work donated by the students and faculty. The money raised we give to some cause, or scholarship or new equipment."

"Then the gang will drift over to my place for drinks, dancing. The whole affair keeps going toward morning. Next day it's breakfast as usual, lots of farewells, tears and embraces, and off they go. Then we've got only two days to clean up for a whole new class. It goes on like this all summer long."

Paulus Berensohn was starting a special lecture in the ceramics studio, and we went to hear it. He had thirty potters posed at their wheels, and the first exercise was a series of small pots quickly thrown within a minute's time. "Most beginners," Paulus had explained, "are too conservative; they won't take chances. This method relaxes them." Paulus paced the studio, stopwatch in hand. He is a former professional dancer and moves with dancer's grace.

Six years ago, Paulus gave up making pots to devote his full time to teaching ceramics and writing. He began *Finding One's Way With Clay* at Penland and dedicated the book to Bill Brown.

"Try to relax," Paulus instructed, "close your eyes, take a deep breath . . ." He paced softly between the rows of wheels, a short man, long-haired and striking-looking. His brown eyes seep up everything in sight, dominate his face. "Think of your insides . . . deep in your insides, as a bowl of Jello . . . a full bowl of Jello." A few people begin to laugh at the metaphor, people relax finally, sigh. "Begin!"

For ten quick minutes they race through the exercises, producing ten small pots. His instructions are quick and simple. "Cut from the wheel! . . . Center! . . . Relax! . . . Begin!" There's a rock of noise as wheels are kicked into motion. The clay is gripped by wet hands, shaped and walls begin to form. Everyone is bent over the wheels in work, straining against the time and labor. Paulus paces among them, smiling with his eyes, nursing his pipe.

The silversmiths in the next room are more casual, conversations are carried on across tables. Their work is much more precise, and they are engaged in making pieces of jewelry, small tea strainers, rings. This session is nearly all women, and they are being taught by a woman, Mary Ann Sherr. No one thinks, however, that the interest in metalwork has anything to do with the women's movement. True, they use hammers, vises and torches, but the work itself is refined and careful. They think their interest in silversmithing comes more from the use of jewelry than anything else.

They work steadily all day, then before dinner it's a pick-up game of volleyball or a walk across the fields and through the woods that surround the main buildings. A chance to get out into the hills. After eating, students drift back into their studios for a couple more hours of work. There are always jobs to be done, kilns to be fired, projects to be finished. There's also a nightly lecture or movie in the dining room and, with dusk, the lights are visible again. Penland stands out against Art'ur's Knob.

PART II

The following colleges, workshops, studios and individuals offer craft courses. This is not a comprehensive list—every day new learning opportunities for crafts become available—but we have listed all the possibilities we could find as of spring 1974.

ALABAMA

The *University of South Alabama* in its Department of Art has two types of courses: studio and history of art. They say, "Studio art offers to every student an opportunity for experience and instruction in art techniques," but the course concentrates on ceramics. To obtain a BFA, a student can spend the majority of time within the Department of Art. That's not bad.

Auburn University has a BFA in Fine Arts and Visual Design. Only a few crafts are offered. A fine arts place.

Addresses

Director of Admissions
Auburn University
Auburn, Alabama
36830
205-826-4080

Director of Admissions
University of South Alabama
307 Gaillard Drive
Mobile, Alabama
36688
205-460-6101

Additional Information

Jennie McElhaney
Alabama Craftsmens Council
Montgomery, Alabama
36106
205-264-1752

Alabama State Council on
the Arts
513 Madison
Montgomery, Alabama
36104
205-269-7804

Lakin Boyd
American Crafts Council
P.O. Box 43
Normal, Alabama
35762

Mrs. Franklin Collier
P.O. Box 6125
Montgomery, Alabama
36106

Kathleen Skurka
1569-A Dunbar Street
Montgomery, Alabama
36106

Lowell Vann
3472 Birchtree Drive
Birmingham, Alabama
35226

Eugenia Lemon
1201 Marseille Drive
Mobile, Alabama
36609

Additional Information (Cont.)

Rhea Smith
1109-8th Avenue
Selma, Alabama
36701

ALASKA

Way up there in Alaska, in Sitka, is *Sheldon Jackson College.* The Department of Fine Arts offers courses in ceramics, basic and intermediate, but there is not much to them. Sheldon Jackson is a two-year, religiously related school, coeducational, and awards only an AA degree.

Addresses

Director of Admissions
Sheldon Jackson College
Box 479
Sitka, Alaska
99835
907-747-5231

Additional Information

A. James Bravar
Alaska State Council on the Arts
Mackay Building
338 Denali Street
Anchorage, Alaska
99501
907-279-3824

ARIZONA

The *Pendleton Shop* is a small privately owned weaving studio. They offer two-week concentrated courses throughout the year and are only looking for serious students. Instruction includes all phases of handweaving, from the planning to the finished fabric. They also offer tapestry techniques, draft writing, fabric analysis and other related subjects. Mary Pendleton, who owns the shop, is a famous teacher who has taught handweaving for twenty-five years. She also edits the national publication, *The Looming Arts*. Pendleton couldn't be located in a nicer spot. It's in the red-rock country of Sedona and Oak Creek Canyon. The studios are new and air-conditioned. Mary says they're "refrigerated air-conditioned." Classes are all day, Monday through Friday.

In Prescott, *Yavapai College* has a strong program in crafts, particularly ceramics and a new class in glassblowing. It is a good place to begin work in crafts. They have a new art building for the craft classes and use a local bronze casting foundry for bronze casting. The staff of this two-year college is mostly part-time, only three full-time instructors. Instruction is competent. They at least concentrate on crafts in this art department.

At *Arizona State University* you can earn all sorts of degrees, BFAs and MFAs, but this is chiefly a teachers college. At the undergraduate level students divide their time between a large core curriculum and the area of specialization. The thrust of the craft offerings is toward ceramics, with a few odd courses in jewelry and textiles. The Art Department is not that committed to crafts.

In Flagstaff, at *Northern Arizona University,* they have a College of Creative Arts with courses in crafts that lead to a major. The range of crafts is metal, textiles, ceramics and some wood sculpture. Lots of required core courses need to be taken, but most are classes you'd want to take. The school is growing quickly, has two campuses, lots of new buildings and equipment.

The *University of Arizona* has both a BFA and an MFA. It offers ceramics, metal, jewelry and silversmithing. Courses are arranged to get students education degrees. This is a big college, not very close, and instruction is straight.

One last school is *Arizona Western College* in Yuma. In their Fine Arts Department they have courses in ceramics and jewelry, and some general craft courses. Not much.

Crane Station in Tucson is an excellent place for weavers. They give instruction in all aspects of weaving. Classes are taught by Crane Day who has taught in colleges all over the United States. Good place to begin.

Addresses

Director of Admissions
Arizona State University
Tempe, Arizona
85281
602-965-9011

Director of Admissions
Arizona Western College
P.O. Box 929
Yuma, Arizona
85364
602-726-1000

Crane Station
3025 North Campbell Avenue
Tucson, Arizona
85719
602-327-0512

Director of Admissions
Northern Arizona University
Flagstaff, Arizona
86001
602-523-9011

The Pendleton Shop
Handweaving Studio
Box 233
Jordan Road
Sedona, Arizona
86336
602-282-3671

Director of Admissions
University of Arizona
Tucson, Arizona
85721
602-884-3237

Director of Admissions
Yavapai College
1100 East Sheldon Street
Prescott, Arizona
86301
602-445-7300

Additional Information

Executive Director
Arizona Commission on the Arts
6330 North Seventh Street
Phoenix, Arizona
85014
602-271-5884

ARKANSAS

A few colleges in Arkansas have classes in crafts. *Arkansas State University* has a BFA degree, but the courses are heavy with requirements and geared toward teaching. The only real craft offering is ceramics. At *Southern State College* you can pick up courses in ceramics and enameling, but no major. *Harding*

College, a very religious place (there's daily chapel) has craft courses—they recommend the courses for camp counselors so you can see what level it is—in ceramics and metal work.

In Little Rock at the *Arkansas Art Center* there's a more than adequate offering of craft courses. These are given in two twelve-week semesters and a summer session of eight weeks. There are courses in all aspects of ceramics, also enameling and a basic course in glassblowing. This is an active art center.

A variety of fairs are held in Arkansas during a long summer and fall. The most famous is the *Ozark Arts and Crafts Fair* held on War Eagle Mills Farm in Hindsville during the month of June. There they hold outdoor classes at the same time in pottery, woodcutting and weaving. This is intensive stuff with excellent instructors. Willard Stone, one of the finest wood sculptors in America, has taught here. In October the Ozarks Crafts Fair is held, the largest market for handcrafted goods made in the Ozarks area.

Addresses

Arkansas Art Center
MacArthur Park
Little Rock, Arkansas
72201
501-376-3671

Director of Admissions
Arkansas State University
State University, Arkansas
72467
501-972-2031

Director of Admissions
Harding College
Searcy, Arkansas
72143
501-268-6161

Ozark Arts and Crafts Fair
War Eagle Mills Farm
Route 1
Hindsville, Arkansas
72738
501-789-2540

Director of Admissions
Southern State College
Magnolia, Arkansas
71753
501-234-5120

Additional Information

Abbott Arts and Crafts Club
Abbott, Arkansas
72920

Arkansas Commission on the Arts
Executive Director
Department of Planning
5th Floor Capitol Hill Building
Little Rock, Arkansas
72201
501-371-1211

Mrs. R. E. Lowe, Jr.
Arts and Crafts
111 N. Main
Brinkley, Arkansas
72021

Mrs. Faye Neumann
Arts and Crafts Guild
Avalon Place
Helena, Arkansas
72342

Paul Wolfe, President
Baxter County Arts and Crafts
Association
1024 Maple
Mountain Home, Arkansas
72653

Mona Waymack, Secretary
Brush and Palette Guild
Route 7, Box 564
Pine Bluff, Arkansas
71601

Mrs. L. Mistie, Secretary
Council of Ozark Artists and
Craftsmen
219 W. Willow
Rogers, Arkansas
72756

Leonard Sherman
Designer Craftsmen of Arkansas
1616 N. Taylor
Little Rock, Arkansas
72205

Hugh Hardwick, President
Grand Prairie Brush and Pallette
Club
123 S. Tyler
DeWitt, Arkansas
72042

Mrs. Guner Eruren
Handweavers Guild of America
5913 Hawthorne
Little Rock, Arkansas
72207

Harrison Arts and Crafts
Harrison, Arkansas
72601

Mrs. W. C. Sheppard, President
Hot Springs Ceramic Association
Route 4, Box 288-A
Hot Springs, Arkansas
71901

Mrs. Eugene Mapes
Mid-Southern Watercolorists
622 N. Bryan Street
Little Rock, Arkansas
72205

Townsend Wolfe, Director
Neighborhood Arts Project
Arkansas Arts Center
MacArthur Park
Little Rock, Arkansas
72202

Samuel F. Norris
Norris School of Art
810 W. Walnut
Blytheville, Arkansas
72315

Mrs. Blanche Elliott, Director
Ozark Arts and Crafts Fair
Association
War Eagle Mills
Hindsville, Arkansas
72738

Mrs. Leota Hickey, Business
Agent
Ozark Foothills Crafts Guild
908 Sugar Loaf
Heber Springs, Arkansas
72543

Rosalie Bushnok
Pine Bluff Brush and Palette
Guild
3607 Main Street
Pine Bluff, Arkansas
71601

Lyndall Forbes
South Arkansas Art League
Lion Oil Company
El Dorado, Arkansas
71730

Thomas W. Jackson, President
Southern Artists Association
Gallery
Fine Arts Center
815 Whittington
Hot Springs, Arkansas
72901

Barron Stanhope
Texarkana Art Club
Stanhope's Arts Supplies
Texarkana, Arkansas
75501

Mrs. George Molner, Secretary
Why-Knot Weavers
10801 Bainbridge Drive
Little Rock, Arkansas
72201

CALIFORNIA

American River College is a junior college offering an AA degree in metal, jewelry and ceramics. Solid foundation work, but general. *Apple Room* teaches batik and weaving, limited but inexpensive. *Arts and Crafts Cooperative* was started in 1959 by a small group of artists and craftsmen. Classes are in jewelry, pottery, stitchery, non-loom weaving and off-hand glassblowing. They also have a retail store and gallery. This is at the very least a good place to hang out. *Augustine Glass Works* has instruction in all forms of glasswork. Serious and technical and only for serious students.

Barnsdall Art and Crafts Center operates year round and students receive individual instruction. Courses are offered in enameling, jewelry, metal, ceramics, wood, weaving (non-loom and loom), also quilting. Mostly for new students. Instruction is complete. *Berkeley Tapestry Works* is a private weaving school that uses only floor looms. Tapestry weavers work on massive Gobelin tapestry looms. Classes in quilting and non-loom weaving are also possible. Very open and friendly place to learn and work. Students can work at any hour. There's also a six-week course in pattern drafting for beginning students. Go here! *Big Creek Pottery* has courses in the spring, summer, and fall. Instruction is by Bruce McDougal and limited to twenty-four students. The setting is ideal: a ranch sixty miles south of San Francisco. Students live in bunkhouse rooms and are taught all aspects of pottery. No previous experience required. Good place to learn.

Cabrillo College is a small junior college that has some crafts, mainly ceramics and jewelry. Nothing much. *California College of Arts and Crafts* is an outstanding school. They give a wide and solid foundation in arts and crafts, then areas of specialization. A BFA and MFA are given in all major crafts. Tough school to get into, tough to major in crafts. They select students for majors after the sophomore year. One of the best schools in California. *California Institute of the Arts* is a new school, funded by Walt Disney money to be a "professional training ground in the United States encompassing all the visual and performing arts." Crafts are taught here, but really as sculpture. Heavily into the fine arts. First-class college, however.

California State University at Fresno has a BA and MA in crafts—textiles, metals are major areas. This school trains teachers. *California State College at Fullerton* has a BFA and MFA. The major studio areas are ceramics, jewelry, metal, weaving. They train a lot of art teachers here and the emphasis is on the fine arts, but the number of craft courses is large and good facilities are available. Otherwise, it's not an exciting place. *California State College at Long Beach* has a BA and MA also. Small selection of crafts: jewelry, silversmithing, ceramics, textiles. Program is limited. *California State College at Los Angeles* has it all, a BA and MA in all the crafts. Fine program. Structured and full of requirements, but otherwise okay. One of the best.

California State Polytechnic College has some courses in its Art Department: plastics, silversmithing, jewelry, ceramics and wood. They have also a new craft center, a huge workshop in the student union. One of the real nice such operations. *Cane and Basket Supply Company* does have a course in chair caning. That's it! *Casa de las Tejedoras* teaches small classes in weaving, spinning, needlepoint, macramé and tapestry. Mostly hobby stuff.

Chico State College offers a BA and MA, major areas are glass-blowing, ceramics and weaving. Solid stuff. The *College of Marin*, a junior college, has an AA in ceramics, also courses in glassblowing, metal, jewelry and weaving. Basic instruction.

The *Craft School* in Anaheim is offering classes for beginners. Courses are directed into three areas: Casting—instructing student in lost wax processes: carving, spruing, investing, burnout, casting and finishing; fabrication—basics of jewelry construction; sawing, soldering, forging, stone setting and finishing; leather—understanding of contemporary leather techniques; sewing, forming, finishing. *Creative Arts Group* is a collection of artists/craftsmen in Sierra Madre. They teach most crafts, all for new students.

De Anza Community College has beginning classes, a wide selection but only for starters. *Denwar Ceramics* is run by Jo and Esther Dendel; both are well known for their mosaics and writings. They offer short workshops in needlepoint, finger weaving, batik, tie dye and mosaics. Wonderful people and teachers. *Dominican College* of San Rafael has just plastics, enameling, wood and weaving. It's a small, Catholic, co-ed place and has little to offer the craftsman.

Earth, Air, Fire, Water is a month-long course for serious students of ceramics. The course is limited to forty people. All aspects of the craft are covered. The setting is in the Sierra Nevadas. *El Camino College* is a junior college that offers an AA in jewelry and ceramics. Limited. The *Fred Wilson Muddy Wheel Pottery School* has ceramics, weaving and macramé. They also have an apprentice program for students fourteen to twenty-five. One of the few such programs.

Gavilan College has a scattering of classes: silversmithing, jewelry, ceramics, wood, weaving. No major offered. *Ginger Dunlap Pottery* has pottery instruction. Good for beginners. *Hallie's Alley* is a jewelry school with individual instruction. They teach all the latest techniques. And they take only eight students at a time.

Hartnell College has majors in metal, jewelry and ceramics. Small college. *Holy Names College* is a small Catholic college, mostly taught by nuns. They have a BA in ceramics and crafts in general. Nothing much. *Humboldt State College* has a strong program in metal and ceramics. They offer an MA in both.

Ida Grae Weaving Workshop teaches non-loom and loom weaving, spinning and dyeing, design. Also, tapestry, rug and garment design. Classes are very small—four to six—and inexpensive. Sound instruction. *Laguna Beach School of Art* offers a BFA in ceramics, also silversmithing and jewelry. Better than average art school. Fine facilities. *Los Angeles Valley College* has just a major in ceramics, some jewelry. Nothing really. The *Loft* offers classes in floor loom weaving, tapestry loom weaving and inkle loom weaving. Taught by two women long experienced in textiles.

McGroarty Cultural Art Center is run by the Department of Recreation and Parks of Los Angeles. Various crafts are taught, all hobby level. *Mendocino Art Center* is a small, non-profit organization. They have studio work in pottery, weaving, jewelry, glassblowing, needlepoint. In 1970 they established a Resident Art Experience Program, with students living in apartments on the art center ground. Limited to twelve students who can stay for nine months. Good place to study crafts.

Mills College has a Fine Art Department, which offers an MA in ceramics. Lovely campus. *Modesto Junior College* has a small Art Department, some crafts: ceramics, jewelry and metal. That's all and not much. *New College of California* at Sausalito, an experimental college, has developed an apprentice program for its students. Just beginning and limited.

Otis Art Institute is a very fine art school in Los Angeles. One of the better private institutions. A BFA in art is offered and an MFA in ceramics is possible. All crafts are taught, but this is really a fine arts place.

Palomar Community College is a two-year college with some crafts. Introductory stuff. They do have glassblowing, however. *Pasadena City College* is another two-year place. They have jewelry and textiles, other general crafts. *Pepperdine University* with campuses in Los Angeles and Malibu has some crafts in their Department of Communication Arts, all general classes except for several courses in ceramics. The Malibu campus does a bit better, glassblowing is taught here. *Porterville College* is a community college. They teach general crafts, jewelry.

The *Pot Shop* has classes in ceramics, some basic instruction in weaving. Beginner's instruction and solid. Good folk. *The Pottery* has just courses in ceramics. Limited. The *Pottery Workshop* is small and informal. All courses are taught and all methods: pinch, coil, mold, etc. "Pond Farm" method of throwing is taught on the kickwheels. This is a good place to begin.

Richard Art Center has some crafts: jewelry, ceramics, textiles, weaving, stitchery, plastics. Hobby level generally. *Rio Hondo College* has introductory classes in glassblowing, ceramics and weaving. Look elsewhere.

Sacramento State College has an AB, BS and MS in ceramics. Strong in this craft only, few other crafts are taught. *San Diego Mesa Junior College* offers only a few classes in jewelry and ceramics. *San Diego State College* has an AB in enameling, metal, jewelry, ceramics, weaving, plastics. But nothing really worthwhile.

San Fernando Valley State College has only silversmithing, ceramics, wood and weaving. Nothing too serious. The *College of the San Francisco Art Institute* is a fine arts place, but they have a major in sculpture/ceramics; a school for artists. *San Francisco Academy of Art College* has a BFA in plastics, metal and wood. Another fine arts place. *San Joaquin Delta College* has ceramics only. *San Jose State College* has a BA and MA in ceramics and crafts in general. All crafts are taught; it's a big arts and crafts program. Name it, they have it! *Santa Barbara Art Institute* has a BFA in ceramics and glassblowing. This institute leans toward fine arts, but it's a first class place. *Scripps College* is the women's college in the Claremont Colleges complex. A BA is possible in ceramics, textile design and weaving. Very good college. A nice place to attend school.

Straw into Gold has courses in weaving, spinning and dyeing. This is a tools and supplies place and they teach on the side. Nice folk. *Studio West* is an extremely interesting place; they write, "We seek to equip the participant with sufficient background in his craft so that he may perform as a self-sufficient artist." There are no admission deadlines, grades or class schedules. Admissions depends on "promise, dedication and maturity." Studio West is based on a strong Christian ethic. "We do not partake in alcohol, tobacco, or any other means which would cause the individual to lessen control over himself." Crafts taught are: ceramics, weaving, wood cabinetry and furniture. No more than two apprentices at a time to a craftsman/artisan.

William Tapia teaches bookbinding classes only. Students start at any time and progress at their own speed. Tapia teaches by strict European standards. All instruction is individual.

The *University of California at Berkeley* has in their College of Environmental Design some craft courses, but they're phasing them out. Avoid the place. The *University of California at Davis* has a BA and MFA in ceramics, also a BA in metal. The *University of California in Los Angeles* has an MA and MFA in glass, ceramics, textiles and weaving. Very good place. At the *University of Redlands* there's jewelry, ceramics, wood and weaving, but the Art Department is really only for fine arts. The *University of Southern California* has only glassblowing, metal and ceramics. At the *University of the Pacific* there's a wide range of crafts: enameling, metal, jewelry, ceramics, wood, weaving, stitchery. But no degree.

Vesta's Studio is run by Vesta Ward. She teaches weaving, stitchery, jewelry and rug making. Good for beginners. *Woman's Workshop* offers a lot more (and for men too) but the courses are all short, and mostly at the hobby level. The *Yarn Depot, Inc.* teaches basic courses for beginners in all aspects of fabrics. Very useful classes. *Yuba College* is a community college that has jewelry, ceramics, weaving and spinning. Nothing much. Joseph Young's *Art in Architecture* is concerned with mosaics in relation to the environment. Students work in fresco, stained glass, mosaics, cast bronze, carved stone and tapestry. A unique place and opportunity.

One special apprenticeship service program is directed for high school students at *Pacific High School* in L.A. This program sets up craft apprenticeships for young people. Pacific High is a very fine alternative form of education; write them. They are looking for students and teachers.

Another fine Apprenticeship Program for *anyone* is with

the *Baulines Craftsman's Guild* in Bolinas. The Baulines Craftsman's Guild came into existence in the spring of 1971 for the explicit purpose of offering full-time apprenticeships in crafts fields. The Baulines Guild (Baulines means "whale" and is the original Portuguese word for the town) is a non-profit educational group of 21 master craftsmen and ten apprentices.

One can join the Guild as an apprentice by writing the coordinator and indicating a field of interest. A meeting is then established between the inquiring apprentice and the master craftsman. All the details are worked out in a personal way. The center of the entire program is on a one-to-one relationship between the master craftsman and his or her apprentice.

The cost per month for an apprenticeship for everything— housing, food, instruction—is about $350.00. The Guild is unhappy about the high cost of instruction and is making efforts to gain scholarship aid from several foundations. Write these people!

Addresses

Director of Admissions
American River College
4700 College Oak Drive
Sacramento, California
95841
916-484-8011

Director
Apple Room
510 North Hoover Street
Los Angeles, California
90004
213-664-1534

Joseph Young
Art in Architecture
8422 Melrose Avenue
Los Angeles, California
90069
213-653-1194

Arts and Crafts Cooperative
1652 Shattuck Avenue

Berkeley, California
94709
415-843-2527

Director
Augustine Glass Works
929 B Pico Boulevard
Santa Monica, California
90405
213-394-5181

Barnsdall Art and Craft Center
4800 Hollywood Boulevard
Los Angeles, California
90027
213-661-6369

Baulines Craftsman's Guild
Tom D'Onofrio
Box 305
Bolinas, California
94924
415-868-1726

Addresses (Cont.)

Berkeley Tapestry Works
1940 Bonita Avenue
Berkeley, California
94704
415-548-7080

Big Creek Pottery
Davenport, California
95017
408-423-4402

Director of Admissions
Cabrillo College
6500 Soquel Drive
Aptos, California
95003
408-475-6000

Director of Admissions
California College of Arts and
Crafts
5212 Broadway
Oakland, California
94618
415-653-8118

Director of Admissions
California Institute of the Arts
Valencia, California
91355
805-255-1050

Director of Admissions
California State College at
Fresno
Fresno, California
93710
209-487-2261

Director of Admissions
California State College at
Fullerton
Fullerton, California
92634
714-870-2011

Director of Admissions
California State College at Long
Beach

6101 East Seventh Street
Long Beach, California
90801
213-498-4144

Director of Admissions
California State College at Los
Angeles
5151 State College Drive
Los Angeles, California
90032
213-224-3361

Director of Admissions
California State Polytechnic
College
San Luis Obispo, Caalifornia
93401
805-546-0111

Cane and Basket Supply Company
1283 South Cochran Avenue
Los Angeles, California
90019
213-939-9644

Casa de las Tejedoras
1619 East Edinger
Santa Ana, California
92705
714-541-0711

Director of Admissions
Chico State College
Chico, California
95926
916-345-6116

Director of Admissions
College of Marin
Kentfield, California
94904
415-454-3962

Craft School
1419 North Central Park Avenue
Anaheim, California
92802
714-535-0776

Creative Arts Group
37 East Montecito
Sierra Madre, California
91024
213-355-8350

Director of Admissions
De Anza Community College
21250 Stevens Creek Boulevard
Cupertino, California
94601
408-257-5550

Denwar Ceramics
236 East Sixteenth Street
Costa Mesa, California
92627
714-548-1342

Director of Admissions
Dominican College
San Rafael, California
94901
415-453-1047

Earth, Air, Fire, Water
Route 2
Box 1930
Grass Valley, California
95945
No Phone

Director of Admissions
El Camino College
16007 Crenshaw Boulevard
Torrance, California
90506
213-324-6631

Director of Admissions
Gavilan College
5055 Santa Teresa Boulevard
Gilroy, California
95020
408-842-8221

Ginger Dunlap Pottery
514 North Hoover Street

Los Angeles, California
90004
213-666-7966

Hallie's Alley
13045 Ventura Boulevard
Studio City, California
91604
213-986-1975

Director of Admissions
Hartnell College
156 Homestead
Salinas, California
93901
408-422-9606

Director of Admissions
Holy Names College
3500 Mountain Boulevard
Oakland, California
94619
415-436-0111

Director of Admissions
Humboldt State College
Arcata, California
95521
707-826-3621

Ida Grae Weaving Workshop
424 LaVerne Avenue
Mill Valley, California
94941
415-388-6101

Laguna Beach School of Art
630 Laguna Canyon Road
Laguna Beach, California
92651
714-494-1520

The Loft
Folklorico Yarn Company
522 Ramona Street
Palo Alto, California
415-327-6302

Addresses (Cont.)

Director of Admissions
Los Angeles Valley College
5800 Fulton Avenue
Van Nuys, California
91401
213-781-1200

McGroarty Cultural Art Center
7570 McGroarty Terrace
Tujunga, California
91042
213-352-5285

Mendocino Art Center
P.O. Box 36
Mendocino, California
95460
707-937-5229

Director of Admissions
Mills College
Oakland, California
94613
415-632-2700

Director of Admissions
Modesto Junior College
College Avenue
Modesto, California
95350
209-524-1451

Fred Wilson
Muddy Wheel Pottery School
12954 Ventura Boulevard
Studio City, California
91604
213-783-3948

Director of Admissions
New College of California
P.O. Box 248
Sausalito, California
94965
415-332-6900

Director of Admissions
Otis Art Institute

2410 Wilshire Boulevard
Los Angeles, California
90057
213-387-5288

Pacific High School
Apprenticeship Service Program
12100 Skyline Boulevard
Los Angeles, California
95030
408-867-2260

Director of Admissions
Palomar Community College
Mission Road
San Marcos, California
92069
714-744-1150

Director of Admissions
Pasadena City College
1570 East Colorado Boulevard
Pasadena, California
91106
213-795-6961

Director of Admissions
Pepperdine University
8035 South Vermont Avenue
Los Angeles, California
90044
213-753-1414

Director of Admissions
Porterville College
900 South Main Street
Porterville, California
93257
209-781-3130

Pot Shop
324 Sunset Avenue
Venice, California
90291
213-399-9714

The Pottery
5838 Perry Drive
Culver City, California
90230
213-836-8808

Pottery Workshop
110 A Camino Pablo
Orinda, California
94563
415-254-5252

Richmond Art Center
Civic Center Plaza
Richmond, California
94804
415-234-2397

Director of Admissions
Rio Hondo College
3600 Workman Mill Road
Whittier, California
90608
213-692-0921

Director of Admissions
Sacramento State College
6000 J Street
Sacramento, California
95814
916-454-6011

Director of Admissions
San Diego Mesa Junior College
7250 Artillery Drive
San Diego, California
92111
714-279-2300

Director of Admissions
San Diego State College
College Avenue
San Diego, California
92115
714-286-6871

Director of Admissions
San Fernando Valley State College
18111 Nordhoff Street

Northridge, California
91324
213-885-2968

Director of Admissions
San Francisco Academy of Art
College
625 Sutter Street
San Francisco, California
94102
415-673-4200

Director of Admissions
San Francisco Art Institute
800 Chestnut Street
San Francisco, California
94133
415-771-7020

Director of Admissions
San Joaquin Delta College
Kensington and Alpine
Stockton, California
95204
209-466-2631

Director of Admissions
San Jose State College
Washington Square
San Jose, California
95112
408-272-2000

Santa Barbara Art Institute
2020 Alameda Padre Serra
Santa Barbara, California
93103
805-963-4306

Director of Admissions
Scripps College
Claremont, California
91711
714-626-8511

Straw into Gold
5550 College
Oakland, California
94618
415-654-8359

Addresses (Cont.)

Studio West
167 Saxony
Encinitas, California
92024
714-753-8186

William Tapia Bindery
7513 Melrose Avenue
Los Angeles, California
90046
213-653-0071

Director of Admissions
University of California at
Berkeley
234 Worster Hall
Berkeley, California
94720
415-642-6000

Director of Admissions
University of California at Davis
Davis, California
95616
916-752-1011

Director of Admissions
University of California at Los
Angeles
Los Angeles, California
90024
313-825-4321

Director of Admissions
University of the Pacific
Stockton, California
95204
209-946-2011

Director of Admissions
University of Redlands
1200 Cotton Avenue
Redlands, California
92373
714-793-2121

Director of Admissions
University of Southern California
University Park
Los Angeles, California
90007
213-746-2311

Vesta's Studio
2011 North Greengrove Street
Orange, California
92665
714-637-4888

Woman's Workshop
17042 Devonshire
Northridge, California
91324
213-363-1112

Yarn Depot, Inc.
545 Sutter Street
San Francisco, California
94102
415-362-0501

Director of Admissions
Yuba College
Beale Road at Linda Avenue
Maryville, California
95901
916-742-7351

Individual Instruction

BOOKBINDER
Robert Bruckman
Box 96
Inverness, California
94501

Capricornus
P.O. Box 98
Berkeley, California
94701

Peter Fahey
2859 Sacramento Street
San Francisco, California
94115

Barbara Hiller
4072-20th Street
San Francisco, California
94115

Margaret Lacky
University of California
Extension
Los Angeles, California
90024

Stella Patri
68 Divisadero Street
San Francisco, California
94117

ENAMELING

Mary Scharp
6219 Alviso Avenue
Los Angeles, California
90043

PRINTMAKER

Bettymae Anderson
1028 Mission Street
South Pasadena, California
91030

WEAVING

Lydia Hillier
P.O. Box 85
Manhattan Beach, California
90266

Conny Koning
4207 Manuella Avenue
Palo Alto, California
94306

Libby Platus
1359 Holmby Avenue
Los Angeles, California
90024

Marie Walling
4409 Bakman Avenue
North Hollywood, California
91602

Additional Information

Executive Director
California Arts Commission
808 "O" Street
Sacramento, California
95814
916-445-1530

CANADA

Canada has a number of excellent places to study crafts, both in established colleges and individual studios. One wonderful place for weaving is the *Albion Hills Farm School,* open year round—and with a special summer school. The farm school is thirty-four miles northwest of Toronto, in a Victorian farm house built about 1870 and on 150 acres of farm land. The school raises its own sheep. Twelve students are admitted per session. Spinning, dyeing and weaving are taught. The *Artists' Workshop* in Toronto has some craft courses, but mainly hobby levels. The Workshop is connected with the *New School of Art* which does much better. The New School of Art in Toronto is a privately owned, accredited school that opened in 1965. This place is trying experimentally to improve art education. The school is owned and operated by the students themselves. At this time New School is focused on fine art education but there is a place here for crafts, especially ceramics, and the interest is growing. An open, free and non-structured place. *Notre Dame University of Nelson* has a BFA program, but only offers major in ceramics. This is a fine arts department and hasn't much to give the craftsman.

Lilly Bohlin has a handweaving school in British Columbia. She recently moved to Canada after teaching for twenty years in Ireland and now teaches part-time at the Banff Centre School of Fine Arts besides teaching at her own workshop. She teaches various techniques, including double and triple weave, lace weave, rug weave, traditional and free weave and hangings, pattern weaves, spaced warps, plain and twill weave. Good place to study.

Rozynska Pottery is a summer pottery school in the province of Quebec. Classes are given by Wanda Rozynska, a well-known potter and teacher. All instruction is on an individual basis and the atmosphere is free and relaxed. Excellent summer school opportunity.

The *Banff Centre School of Fine Arts* has an extended summer program and offers a diploma in certain areas. Crafts given are ceramics and weaving. This is mainly a fine arts place, but craft education is growing. Can't go wrong here; a lovely place to attend school for a spring, summer or fall.

Nova Scotia College of Art and Design is the best place for craftsmen in Canada. They offer a BA in Fine Arts and Design. Crafts are wood, metal, ceramics, jewelry, weaving. Very well equipped place. This is a famous (and well deserving of it) school. Large faculty and many visiting craftsmen/lecturers from Europe and the US. Check it out.

Sheridan College is a community school in Ontario that has a school of design and extensive studio work in ceramics, glass metal, jewelry, fabrics and furniture design. Students do a foundation year in all areas, then in the second and third years they concentrate. Another outstanding place to study crafts.

Another small summer program in crafts is at *Elliot Lake* in Ontario. Mostly hobby level, however. A continuing education center that's okay for those who want to learn a craft during a summer vacation.

Addresses

Albion Hills Farm School
R.R. No. 3
Caledon East
Ontario, Canada
416-594-0064

Artists' Workshop
296 Brunswick Avenue
Toronto, 179
Canada
416-920-8370

Banff Centre School of Fine Arts
Banff
Alberta, Canada
403-762-3391

Lilly Bohlin
1021 Government Street
Victoria
British Columbia, Canada
604-388-6308

Director
Elliot Lake
Box 97
Ontario, Canada
705-848-7121

New School of Art
296 Brunswick Avenue

Toronto, 179
Canada
416-920-8370

Registrar
Notre Dame University of Nelson
Nelson
British Columbia, Canada
604-352-2241

Nova Scotia College of Art and Design
6152 Coburg School
Halifax
Nova Scotia, Canada
902-429-1600

Rozynska Pottery
Way's Mills
R.R. 1
Ayer's Cliff
Quebec, Canada
819-838-4321

Registrar
Sheridan College
1430 Trafalgar Road North
Oakville
Ontario, Canada
416-845-9430

COLORADO

In this state there are two colleges that are worthwhile for crafts. The Department of Art at *Colorado State University* has a BFA program in Fine Arts. A student can emphasize ceramics, metalworking and jewelry, or weaving. Students do, however, have to take about half the course work in general studies or electives. Colorado State is a big school, close to 20,000, but it is a fun place to attend. Students come here from all over.

Also very good is *Southern Colorado State* in Pueblo. The Art Department is located in a new building which houses fine new facilities including a slide library and a 2,000 foot gallery. The faculty numbers about eleven, each teaching some area of specialization. Craft courses are jewelry and metalwork, ceramics and wood. The Department of Art has just revised the curriculum to emphasize studio work and courses more directly related to job careers.

At the *University of Northern Colorado* in the School of the Arts there's a major in crafts. At the moment that's ceramics. Very structured with one major area of emphasis—at least 12 quarter hours—and lots of "fine" art classes. You get a teacher's certification. Can't really be recommended.

Elsewhere in Colorado the *University of Colorado* in Boulder has a few courses in ceramics and jewelry design. That's it! In Sterling there's *Northeastern Junior College* with some beginning courses in ceramics. *Western State College* in Gunnison has a bit wider range of courses. There's ceramics, jewelry, weaving and woodcarving. No degree offered.

The *Weaving Shop* offers all levels of instruction into harness weaving, four-harness weaving, multiple harness weaving, card, inkle and finger weaving, also natural dyeing. They have everything here!

Loretto Heights College is a small co-ed place, private, that has developed a new core program and other innovative class structures. They offer a Fine Arts degree and students can take ceramics, metals, jewelry. Mostly a fine arts place, however.

Addresses

Director of Admissions
Colorado State University
Fort Collins, Colorado
80521
303-491-1101

Director of Admisssions
Loretto Heights College
3001 South Federal
Denver, Colorado
80236
303-922-4011

Director of Admissions
Northeastern Junior College
Sterling, Colorado
80751
303-522-6600

Director of Admissions
Southern Colorado State
Pueblo, Colorado
81005
303-545-4220

Director of Admissions
University of Colorado
Boulder, Colorado
80302
303-443-2211

Director of Admissions
University of Northern Colorado
Greeley, Colorado
80631
303-351-1890

The Weaving Shop
1708 Walnut Street
Boulder, Colorado
80302
303-443-1133

Director of Admissions
Western State College
Gunnison, Colorado
81230
303-943-0120

Additional Information

Mrs. Jean Peterson
Colorado Artist Craftsmen
1327 East Cornell
Englewood, Colorado
80110

Executive Director
Colorado Commission on the Arts
1550 Lincoln Street
Denver, Colorado
80203
303-892-2618

CONNECTICUT

The *Brookfield Craft Center* between Danbury and New Milford is a fine non-profit educational center devoted to crafts. The school occupies three buildings on the banks of the Still River—a restored grist mill built about 1950, a separate weaving studio and a large 19th-century barn.

The mill contains the metalsmithing and enameling shops, a large, light river-level studio for classes and lectures. The weaving shop has looms of all kinds and sizes. The barn contains the woodworking shop and the pottery.

Classes are open to anyone age 16 or over and enrollment is limited, so apply early. There are classes in stitchery, weaving, thread construction, frame loom weaving, stained glass, ceramics, woodworking for beginners and contemporary quilting. Classes are not held in all crafts at all times. There are also many many special events, lectures, demonstrations. A great place to be involved with.

The *Pulpit Rock Community for Artists* is in Woodstock, Connecticut, and though at the moment it doesn't take craftsmen, those artists involved with fine arts should know about it. Margaret Tourtellotte, President of the Board, described the place this way: "The underlying feature of our Community is that we provide free studios to artists who qualify in promising talent and compatible character. Our members come mainly just out of art schools and stay with us an average of two years. They then either settle in their own studios in the area or go on to the outside world. The studios are in converted barns on my farm, the barns belonging to my son who gives us the use of them. The artists must find living quarters removed from the studios. This avoids personality problems. They usually become very close friends and there develops a fine community feeling which grows as new artists arrive.

"We have a Board of Directors and we manage all the affairs of the Community. We have been a going Community for six years. Two years were spent in converting the barns. About thirty-seven artists have been with us and some have achieved wide recognition. We serve a much needed refuge for the years after art school. We are situated in a beautiful quiet New England town in northeast Connecticut, within an hour's drive of large cities."

Wesleyan Potters is another non-profit learning center for crafts. Classes are held year-round and there are also lectures, exhibits, demonstrations and discussions. All classes are conducted by qualified teachers and the studio space is large and well-equipped. The major adult classes are in batik and tie dye, jewelry, lapidary, leather, pottery, wood sculpture, spinning, stitchery, off-loom weaving and loom weaving, the four-harness techniques. Fees are not high and classes are kept small. A very good craft center.

The *Hartford Art School* is "a fully accredited four year institution dedicated to the education of professional artists." It is a component of the University of Hartford. It is a very well equipped place. Ceramics is the main craft they have to offer. There are two studios equipped with both electric and kick wheels, a small electric kiln, and room enough for storing clay, glazes and other materials.

All students take a foundation year. It's tough: four-hour studios which meet four days per week, plus special events, assigned readings. One student has written about this year, "Foundation year gives the student a chance to use his or her mind to the fullest. This is something no other art school can offer. Technique can always be learned in the following year. Ask yourself which is more important; the idea or the process. . . . Then ask yourself if one had no ideas, could the process follow?" This is a fine school.

The Department of Art at the *University of Bridgeport* has a few courses, mostly in ceramics, plus some general craft courses, but not much here of interest to a crafts person. The *University of Connecticut* offers a BFA in ceramics. This school is heavily into history of art and appreciation, not much studio work for anyone.

Addresses

Mrs. McCaffery
Brookfield Craft Center
Brookfield, Connecticut
06804
203-775-9681

Director of Admissions
Hartford Art School
University of Hartford
200 Bloomfield Avenue

West Hartford, Connecticut
06117
203-523-4811

Pulpit Rock Community for
Artists
Woodstock, Connecticut
06281
203-928-2046

Addresses (Cont.)

Director of Admissions
University of Bridgeport
285 Park Avenue
Bridgeport, Connecticut
06602
203-384-0711

Director of Admissions
University of Connecticut

Storrs, Connecticut
06268
203-386-3137

Wesleyan Potters
350 South Main Street
Middletown, Connecticut
06457
203-347-5925

Individual Instruction

WEAVING

Kate Edgerton
Edgerton's Handcrafts
210 West Town Street
Norwich, Connecticut
06360
203-889-5990

Additional Information

Executive Director
Connecticut Commission on the
Arts
340 Capital Avenue
Hartford, Connecticut
06106
203-566-4770

DELAWARE

The *Delaware Art Museum* is a non-profit place devoted to "promoting the enjoyment and understanding of the arts." They have new studios and small classes—classes are given in pottery, silversmithing, weaving and batiking. There is individual instruction. All classes are once a week and are limited. Good place to begin.

The Department of Art at the *University of Delaware* is a

"studio-oriented department offering the possibility of intensive study." A masters is also possible. To major in one of these disciplines requires a minimum of thirty-six hours in the department. The major crafts offered are ceramics, jewelry, enameling. A good school here, solid instruction.

Addresses

Registrar, Education Department
Delaware Art Museum
2301 Kentmere Parkway
Wilmington, Delaware
19806
302-655-6289

Director of Admissions
University of Delaware
Newark, Delaware
19711
302-738-2000

Additional Information

Executive Director
Delaware State Arts Council
601 Delaware Avenue
Wilmington, Delaware
19801
302-654-3159

DISTRICT OF COLUMBIA

On the edge of historic Georgetown in an 1864 warehouse is the creation of Maxine G. Brown called the *Craftsmen of Chelsea Court*. Opened in 1970, Chelsea Court is both a retail store and working studios for twenty-four craftsmen. It's the first operation of its kind. Maxine Brown has been accused by some of "commercializing" the crafts, but she's a woman who understands the need to improve the marketing of high quality crafts and has done something about it. She has already opened a second Court in the Watergate complex and has plans for a national distribution system for craftsmen with cooperating centers around the country.

At Chelsea Court apprenticeships and classes are offered in ceramics, woodwork, jewelry, textiles and glass. The Court, however, is not primarily a school and classes are offered only on a part-time basis. The Court is important to the craft world because it demonstrates that it is possible for craftsmen to join together and make a commercial living from their skills. Maxine Brown deserves full credit for her hard work and vision.

Also in Georgetown, in a little shop on the corner of 35th Street, is the *Silver Shuttle*. It's owned by two nice little old ladies who teach courses in beginning and intermediate hand-weaving. Courses are offered for ten weeks, one three-hour class per week. They're informal, with the instruction in fundamental principles and practices planned so the beginning weaver will progress rapidly. The ladies teach the traditional methods, with not many new ideas introduced, but the basics are taught well. This is also one of the few weaving shops in the country where a variety of floor looms and table looms are used. Students can get practice on all types.

Eastern Market Pottery is upstairs over the open food market in southeast Washington, a block from Pennsylvania Avenue. This is a grand place to learn pottery. The owner, Bruce Brome, is relaxed and friendly. The studio itself is crowded with equipment, pots, students and rich with the smells from downstairs.

Bruce Brome himself teaches, and has five other professionals who teach one night a week in exchange for space and use of the kilns. Courses run for six weeks, two hours a session, and the studio is open for use at other times. Classes are kept to twelve students or less and total enrollment is only fifty. Anyone can study for as long as they want and some potters have worked out individual arrangements as apprentices with their teachers. That's how Bruce got started. In Washington it's the best place to learn pottery. There's a waiting list, so apply early.

The Art Department of *Federal City College* offers a fine program, the best place to gain a BA in the District. The one problem here is that crafts are limited to ceramics. There are several fine teachers, Robert Vankluyve, who teaches part-time, is just one. At the college it is possible to concentrate on ceramics; you needn't bother about fine art classes. The college has had administration problems and that has touched the Art Department, but students are still free to work. The Art Department gives students a chance to obtain a BA to teach either in elementary or secondary schools, and gives the student a program to allow him or her a chance to become more proficient in one area. That's what makes it such a good place.

The next best place to learn crafts in D.C. is at the *Smithsonian Institution*. Through the Smithsonian Associates a series of workshops are offered once a week (usually in the evening) for ten weeks at a time. The Smithsonian has some outstanding teachers—Ron Goodman, for example, in fabrics and Joan Koslan Schwartz in stitchery. Both are nationally known artist-craftsmen. Unfortunately the Smithsonian has little equipment and few resources. It's not possible to take weaving or pottery there. With little money and help Carolyn Hecker, who directs the program, has done a fine job.

It is possible at the *Catholic University of America* to obtain BA and MFA degrees in crafts, but the work here is limited to ceramics and is in the Division of Art. The master of art degree has reasonable requirements and is a sound but unexciting program.

Elsewhere in Washington, D.C., craft courses can be taken at the *Corcoran School of Art*. It has part-time basic classes in ceramics and printmaking. There are also some good design and drawing courses a craftsman should take advantage of. Crafts at the Corcoran are not that important to the school.

Then there's the *Textile Museum* on "S" street. This used to be a dull place but several years ago they got a new executive director, Anthony Landreau, who opened up the museum to craftsmen of the area, and now the museum is packed with tourists, friends and students. The museum runs lectures and classes in rug appreciation, Florentine embroidery, needlepoint, rug making and creative stitchery. Most of the staff are unfriendly, but once a person gets by them the Textile Museum is a treasure and also the only one of its kind. The museum has an extensive research library (plus a helpful part-time librarian).

There are a few other studios in Washington, most of them upstairs studios, in Georgetown, but they come and go rather rapidly. Most of the craft world in this area is located in the surrounding states and the District serves as the museum for all these craftsmen. The most important museum to craftsmen is the new *Renwick Gallery* of the Smithsonian Institution. This gallery, located near the White House, is devoted to crafts and design.

Addresses

Director of Admissions
The Catholic University of
America
Washington, D.C.
20017
202-635-5300

The Corcoran School of Art
17th and New York Avenue N.W.
Washington, D.C.
20006
202-628-9484

The Craftsmen of Chelsea Court
2902 M Street N.W.
Washington, D.C.
20007
202-338-4588

Eastern Market Pottery
7th and C S.E.
Washington, D.C.
20003
202-544-6669

Director of Admissions
Federal City College
916 G Street N.W.

Washington, D.C.
20001
202-727-1000

Renwick Gallery
National College of Fine Arts
Smithsonian Institution
Washington, D.C.
20560
202-628-4422

The Silver Shuttle
1301 35th Street N.W.
Washington, D.C.
20007
202-338-3789

Associates Craft Classes
Smithsonian Institution
Washington, D.C.
20560
202-381-5157

The Textile Museum
2320 S Street N.W.
Washington, D.C.
20008
202-667-0442

Individual Instruction

WEAVING

Mrs. W. Gardner Lynn
2935 Northampton Street N.W.
Washington, D.C.
20015
202-362-20015

Additional Information

Leroy Washington
Executive Director,
D.C. Commission on the Arts
1329 E Street N.W.
Washington, D.C.
20004
202-629-5123

FLORIDA

The *Ceramic League of Miami School of Crafts* has eight-week classes in ceramics. Classes are kept small, taught by professional potters. Very good place to begin. The *Colson School of Art* has a few courses in metal and ceramics, that's all. Avoid. The *Florida Gulf Coast Art Center* has ceramics, wood, stitchery, enameling and jewelry. Classes are once a week for ten weeks. This is a beginner's place. *Longboat Key Art Center* is another hobby place, someplace to start. Classes in metal, ceramics, weaving, enameling are offered. The *Miami Art Center* has classes through the year in ceramics and enameling; this is mostly a fine arts place. Go elsewhere. The *Norton Gallery and School of Art* has ceramics, little else for the craftsman. Instruction is by Juanita May, a known potter.

Among colleges, *Barry College* in Miami Shores, a small Catholic place, has some crafts, but really not anything worthwhile. *Daytona Beach Community College* has some general crafts, also not worthwhile. *Florida A & M University* in Tallahassee does a bit better, but still their crafts—plastics, enameling, metal, ceramics, textiles—aren't enough for a degree. *Miami-Dale Junior College* has some introductory courses in half a dozen crafts. Nothing special offered. *Eckerd College* offers clay, jewelry, weaving and woodworking. Courses are offered irregularly, however. Also possible here to do independent study with local craftsmen.

The universities in Florida do much better by craft students. At Gainesville the *University of Florida* has a BFA in plastics, enameling, metal and ceramics. Good program with a large faculty and new facilities. At the *University of Maimi* a BA, BFA and MFA are available in ceramics and weaving. Extensive program, everything you'd want. Recommended. Solid work also in Tampa at the *University of South Florida*. Possible to get a BA in crafts and a MFA in ceramics. Lots of required courses, but the school is designed to produce professionals.

Addresses

Director of Admissions
Barry College
11300 N.E. 2nd Avenue
Miami Shores, Florida
33156
305-758-3392

Ceramic League of Miami School
of Crafts
8873 S.E. 129th Street
Miami, Florida
33156
305-235-9732

Colson School of Art
1666 Hillview
Sarasota, Florida
33579

Director of Admissions
Daytona Beach Community
College
P.O. Box 1111
Daytona Beach, Florida
32015
904-252-9671

Director of Admissions
Eckerd College
P.O. Box 12560
St. Petersburg, Florida
33733
813-867-1166

Director of Admissions
Florida A & M University
Box 512
Tallahassee, Florida
32307
904-222-8030

Florida Gulf Coast Art Center
111 Manatee Road
Clearwater, Florida
33156
813-584-8634

Longboat Key Art Center
P.O. Box 151
Longboat Key, Florida
33548
813-383-2345

Miami Art Center
7867 North Kendall Drive
Miami, Florida
33156
305-271-8450

Director of Admissions
Miami-Dade Junior College
11380 N.W. 27 Avenue
Miami, Florida
33167
305-274-1179

Norton Gallery and School of Art
Box 2309
West Palm Beach, Florida
33402
305-832-5194

Director of Admissions
University of Florida
Gainesville, Florida
32601
904-392-3261

Director of Admissions
University of Miami
1300 Campo Sano

Coral Gables, Florida
33146
305-284-2211

Director of Admissions
University of South Florida

4202 Fowler Avenue
Tampa, Florida
33620
813-974-2011

Individual Instruction

CERAMICS

Paul and Ginny Anthony
510 Ingleside Avenue
Tallahassee, Florida
32303
904-224-2071

Helen Bennett
940 Lancaster Drive, South
Orlando, Florida
32806
305-422-8859

George Bocz
Star Route Box 95x
Tallahassee, Florida
32304
904-576-5005

Jack Brewer
2100-46th South
St. Petersburg, Florida
33711
813-345-3944

William and Kathleen Clover
2530 Wycliff Drive
Pensacola, Florida
32504
904-476-1637

Frank Colson
1666 Hill View Street
Sarasota, Florida
33579
813-958-4032

Mary Coover
8078 Causeway Blvd

St. Petersburg, Florida
33707
813-345-3303

Barbara Culbertson
4844 Brywill Circle
Sarasota, Florida
33580
813-355-3604

Charles Fager
Rt 4 Box 2016
Lutz, Florida
33549
813-949-5109

Mary Grabill
2927 Florida Avenue
Coconut Grove, Florida
33549

Bob Hodgell
Box 46813
102-22nd Avenue
Pass-A-Grille Beach, Florida
33706
813-360-7744

Juanita May
1953 Tiger Tail Avenue
Coconut Grove, Florida
33133
305-448-8387

Jewell Meredith
Box 338
Longboat Key, Florida
33548

Individual Instruction (Cont.)

Carol Robinson
4401 Midnight Pass
Sarasota, Florida
33581
813-922-4934

ENAMELING

Jeanne Garrison
5911 Shore Acres Drive N.W.
Bradenton, Florida
33505
813-744-8905

Kathleen Hinni
1500 North Orange Avenue
Sarasota, Florida
33577
813-958-7695

Ken Uyemura
4706 Alhambra Circle
Coral Gables, Florida
33146

FIBER

Kathleen Day
10208 Kingfisher Road, East
Bradenton, Florida
33505
813-778-3340

Ruth Jelks
244 Pensacola Road
Venice, Florida
33595
813-488-3141

Suzanne Larson
4901 Commonwealth Drive
Sarasota, Florida
33577
813-924-6650

Evelyn Marx
1750 Benjamin Franklin Drive
Sarasota, Florida
33577
813-388-3330

Mary Motty
227 Day Street
Tallahassee, Florida
32304
904-576-1474

Memphis Wood
12359 Woodside Lane
Jacksonville, Florida
32223
904-268-5464

METAL

Frankie MacDonald
7152 Point of Roocks Circle
Sarasota, Florida
33581
813-924-2409

Wiley Tillman
P.O. Box 12582, University Station
Gainesville, Florida
32601
904-376-2326

WEAVING

Margaret Feingold
5321 Avenida Del Mare
Sarasota, Florida
33577
813-924-8450

Raymond Ferguson
3518 N.W. 29th Street
Gainesville, Florida
32601
904-376-8355

Additional Information

Executive Director
Division of Cultural Affairs
Fine Arts Council of Florida
The Capitol Building
Tallahassee, Florida
32304
904-224-4412

GEORGIA

Berry College is one of those small (1,000 students) southern schools, tucked up in the northwest corner of the state. It has an equally small but adequate Art Department that awards a BA. The program mostly trains teachers. Ceramics is the major craft, some jewelry, and it's possible to take welding and foundry classes. The department has individual studio space in a new building. That's a plus.

Georgia College in Milledgeville has a lot less to offer in crafts. The Art Department is concerned with "the creative, educational, and technical development of the student." They offer one or two craft courses, general type. Avoid the place. *Middle Georgia College* is the same kind of school. A few general courses, nothing here for a crafts person. *Valdosta State* hasn't much either; general courses and, naturally, ceramics.

However, in Macon, *Wesleyan College* offers a lot. They have well-equipped studios, offer a BFA in ceramics and have "ceramics facilities including stoneware, porcelain, and earthware manipulations, and variations on gas, electric, and experimental firing techniques." They have a strong foundation section with design built into it. Classes are small with lots of individualized instruction. Wesleyan is a small place, limited faculty.

Georgia State University offers a bachelors in visual arts, has a few crafts courses, nothing much. The school is located in downtown Atlanta, a city school.

The city of Atlanta has several centers where crafts are taught. This is just for residents and the classes are for beginners. You can take classes in handformed clay, copper enameling, leather, pottery on the wheel, jewelry, weaving and stitchery.

Nothing advanced. You need to contact the *Chastain Arts and Crafts Center* or the *Orchard Knob Arts and Crafts Center*.

One very fine place to study pottery is at *Charles Counts*'s *Rising Fawn* studio. Charles Counts is one of the leading figures in the crafts world and has written extensively on the subject. He's also an outstanding potter and teacher.

Addresses

Dean of Admissions
Berry College
Mount Berry, Georgia
30149
404-232-5374

Chastain Arts and Crafts Center
135 West Wieuca Road, N.W.
Atlanta, Georgia
30342

Charles Counts
Rising Fawn, Georgia
30738

Director of Admissions
Georgia College
Milledgeville, Georgia
31061
912-452-5541

Director of Admissions
Georgia State University
33 Gilmer Street, S.E.
Atlanta, Georgia
30303
404-658-2000

Director of Admissions
Middle Georgia College
Cochran, Georgia
31014
912-934-6221

Orchard Knob Arts and Crafts Center
2055 Humphries Drive, S.E.
Atlanta, Georgia
30315
404-361-4165

Director of Admissions
Valdosta State College
Valdosta, Georgia
31601
912-244-6340

Director of Admissions
Wesleyan College
4760 Forsyth Road
Macon, Georgia
31201
912-477-1110

Additional Information

Arts Section
Georgia Office of Planning
706 Peachtree Center South
Building
225 Peachtree Street, N.E.
Atlanta, Georgia
30303
404-656-3990

HAWAII

In *Honolulu* the *University of Hawaii* has both a BFA and MFA in ceramics, textiles, weaving. There are also classes in other crafts: glassblowing, ceramics, jewelry. The *University of Hawaii at Hilo* has a continuing education program and some crafts are offered, mostly hobby levels.

Addresses

Director of Admissions
Continuing Education
University of Hawaii at Hilo
P.O. Box 1357
Hilo, Hawaii
96720
808-935-4827

Director of Admissions
University of Hawaii at Honolulu
2560 Campus Road
Honolulu, Hawaii
96822
808-948-8111

Additional Information

Mrs. Mirella Belshe,
President
Hawaii Craftsmen
3231 Beaumont Woods Place
Honolulu, Hawaii
96822

Hawaii State Foundation on
Culture and the Arts
Executive Director
250 South King Street
Kamamalu Building
Honolulu, Hawaii
96813
808-548-4145

IDAHO

In *Boise State College* the Department of Art offers a BFA degree for those who want to teach in secondary school. They have general craft courses in the first year of school and it's possible to major in ceramics, but not much beyond that. The faculty is limited, though they have a brand new building and lots of space and equipment.

Idaho State University has a BA and MFA in crafts. It is really a fine arts degree, and they have tacked on some crafts work late in the curriculum. The MFA degree is not much better for craftsmen. Plus it isn't even an attractive college to attend.

The *University of Idaho* in Moscow has courses in ceramics, jewelry and some general crafts. This is mostly a place to train teachers. Not strong in crafts.

Addresses

Director of Admissions
Boise State College
1907 Campus Drive
Boise, Idaho
83707
208-385-1011

Director of Admissions
Idaho State University
741 S. 7th
Pocatello, Idaho
83201
208-236-0211

Director of Admissions
University of Idaho
Moscow, Idaho
83843
208-885-6111

Additional Information

Executive Director
Idaho State Commission on the
Arts
P.O. Box 577
Boise, Idaho
83701
208-384-2119

ILLINOIS

The *Art Institute of Chicago* has a school that offers a BFA and an MFA in glassblowing, ceramics, weaving. All students take a broad based foundation year, then concentrate in the next three years in one craft. There is also a wide range of liberal arts courses to be taken. This is a first-rate school. *Augustana College* is a small religious place, conservative. A BA is given with majors in jewelry, ceramics, weaving, stitchery, but this is a fine arts department. Nothing really here.

Belleville Area College near St. Louis has jewelry and weaving. That's all, and the college isn't worth it. *Burpee Art Museum* offers some introductory classes in jewelry, spinning and dyeing. *College of DuPage* has only enameling and jewelry. Very limited. *College of St. Francis* in Joliet has in the Fine Arts Department some ceramics, weaving and spinning, but this school is more concerned with the history of art than with crafts.

Contemporary Art Workshop is a non-profit and local Chicago organization that has been growing in importance for over twenty years. It began in 1950 in an old Cyrus McCormick carriage barn. Classes are in clay, wood, resin, steel, bronze, stone, but all are geared toward producing sculpture. Studio space is available for craftsmen. This is a serious workshop, and for artists.

Eastern Illinois University has just a few odd courses: ceramics, weaving, plastics and macramé. *Evanston Art Center* has a small school offering some classes in ceramics, weaving, plastics and macramé. Okay to begin here.

The *Hill* near Joliet is an art center that has real possibilities. It is the production studio of a very creative man, Orion Hargett, and he is trying to build in the Joliet area a community for artists and craftsmen. Work space is available for craftsmen working in any and all crafts. This place is more for artists than for someone interested in production. In this area it's the very best.

Illinois State University in Normal has a BS and MS in crafts. You can study glassblowing, metal, jewelry, ceramics and weaving. All of this, however, is geared toward students interested in teaching. *Looms and Lessons* is a small workshop where you can learn weaving. It's conducted by Ruth Nordquist Myers and is run out of her home; mostly individual lessons for beginners.

Mundelein College is a small Catholic women's college. They have a BFA in weaving, stitchery, batik and tie-dye. Limited and a fine arts place. *Northern Illinois University* has a BFA in textile design and their College of Fine and Allied Arts is a particularly good place to study textiles. Also BFAs and MFAs are available in metalwork, jewelry, ceramics and weaving. One of the better places to study in Illinois. Small *Rockford College* has a BA major in ceramics, weaving, batik and spinning, but not much else. *Roosevelt University* downtown in Chicago has some general crafts courses. Nothing really.

Southern Illinois University in Carbondale has both BA and MFA degrees. Specialization is in metal, ceramics and weaving. A broad program, studio space and all the equipment you need. But the campus is unattractive. The *University of Chicago* has some undergraduate craft courses, but it's their MFA in ceramics that counts. Academic and hard, the craft masters is based on theory and history, not for the casual learner.

At the *University of Illinois* in their College of Fine and Applied Arts you can concentrate in ceramics, metalwork or jewelry. The basic program is followed by specialized training. This is an excellent crafts place in these few areas. Can't go wrong here.

Weaving Workshop has some beginning courses in weaving, batik, spinning and dyeing. Good starting point. *Western Illinois University* has an MA in metal, silversmithing, ceramics and weaving. They have very good facilities. Not a bad college. *Wheaton College* offers some odd courses in metal and ceramics.

Addresses

Director of Admissions
Augustana College
Rock Island, Illinois
61201
309-794-7341

Director of Admissions
Belleville Area College
2500 Carlyle Road
Belleville, Illinois
62221
618-235-2700

Burpee Art Museum
737 North Main Street
Rockford, Illinois
61103
815-965-3131

Director of Admissions
College of DuPage
22nd and Lambert Road

Glen Ellyn, Illinois
60540
312-858-4830

Director of Admissions
College of St. Francis
Joliet, Illinois
60435
815-726-7311

Contemporary Art Workshop
542 West Grant Place
Chicago, Illinois
60614
312-525-9624

Director of Admissions
Eastern Illinois University
Charleston, Illinois
61920
217-581-2223

Evanston Art Center
2603 Sheridan Road
Evanston, Illinois
60201
312-475-5300

The Hill
711 Rowell Avenue
Joliet, Illinois
60433
815-727-2641

Director of Admissions
Illinois State University
Hovey Hall
Normal, Illinois
61761
309-438-2111

The School of Art
Institute of Chicago
Michigan Avenue and Adams
Streeet
Chicago, Illinois
60603
312-236-7080, ext. 278

Looms and Lessons
6014 Osage Avenue
Downers Grove, Illinois
60515
312-964-1211

Director of Admissions
Mundelein College
6363 Sheridan Road
Chicago, Illinois
60627
312-262-8100

Director of Admissions
Northern Illinois University
DeKalb, Illinois
60115
815-753-1000

Director of Admissions
Rockford College
5050 State East

Rockford, Illinois
61201
815-226-4000

Director of Admissions
Roosevelt University
430 South Michigan
Chicago, Illinois
60605
312-341-3500

Director of Admissions
Southern Illinois University
Carbondale, Illinois
62901
618-453-4381

Director of Admissions
University of Chicago
Chicago, Illinois
60637
312-753-1234

Director of Admissions
University of Illinois
College of Fine and Applied Arts
Urbana, Illinois
61802
217-333-1000

Weaving Workshop
3324 North Halsted
Chicago, Illinois
60657
312-929-5776

Director of Admissions
Western Illinois University
Macomb, Illinois
61455
309-295-1414

Director of Admissions
Wheaton College
Wheaton, Illinois
60187
312-682-5005

Additional Information

Illinois Arts Council
111 North Wabash Avenue
Chicago, Illinois
60602
312-793-3520

Mr. James Myers
Prairie House
213 South 6th Street
Springfield, Illinois
62701
217-544-2094

INDIANA

Ball State University offers a BA and BS in silversmithing, jewelry, ceramics and weaving. Almost all crafts are given at this small, little-known place. A standard but complete course is offered. *Depauw University* in Greencastle is a very small liberal arts place. They have jewelry and ceramics, nothing serious, though it's a nice old-fashioned kind of college. *Franklin College,* another small place of 700 students, has classes in ceramics and printing. Nothing else. *Herron School of Art* is an old school— 1891—that in 1967 joined with Indiana University and Purdue University to offer degrees. It's a very fine art school that does have some crafts, but craft courses are only offered as electives and for students wanting to be elementary teachers. Good school for basic art design and appreciation.

Indiana State University offers a BS degree in their Art Department. Curriculum is set up for teachers. Studio work is offered in ceramics, jewelry and silversmithing. Basic stuff. *Indiana University* has a huge campus at Bloomington and other branches around the state. They offer everything for a crafts person. There's an AB and BFA in silversmithing and jewelry; AB, BFA and MFA in enameling, textile design, stitchery, batik, weaving. Very good place if you can handle a huge campus and a large college.

Another large campus is *Purdue University.* They have a BA in jewelry, weaving and print and dye. Also a BA and MA in ceramics. They train teachers here. Good in basics and in all aspects of design. *Saint Mary's College* of Notre Dame has a BFA and offers glass, enameling, jewelry, ceramics, weaving. They have an interdepartmental approach to education, requirements and lots of fine arts, but the place is better than the average women's college.

The *University of Evansville* has a BA in textiles, a BFA in crafts, and a BA, BFA and MA in ceramics. The Department of Art is important at the college and a solid degree is given, lots of studio work. Faculty is small, however, and limited.

Other opportunities in the state are: *Craft Kaleidoscope* in Indianapolis. The school teaches handweaving, macramé, spinning and stitchery. Most for beginners. The *Fort Wayne School of Fine Arts* is much more complete. They offer a BFA in metal, jewelry and ceramics. A foundation course is offered, then concentration. Good place. The *Gary Art Center* is similar. They have a BA in plastics, metal, jewelry and stitchery; an MA in ceramics and textiles. Of the three, Fort Wayne School of Fine Arts is the best place.

Addresses

Director of Admissions
Ball State University
Muncie, Indiana
47306
317-289-1241

Craft Kaleidoscope
6551 Ferguson Street
Indianapolis, Indiana
46220
317-251-1035

Director of Admissions
Depauw University
Greencastle, Indiana
46135
317-653-9721

Director of Admissions
Fort Wayne School of Fine Arts
1026 West Berry Street
Fort Wayne, Indiana
46804
219-743-9796

Director of Admissions
Franklin College

Franklin, Indiana
46131
317-736-8441

Director of Admissions
Gary Art Center
400 South Lake Street
Gary, Indiana
46403
219-882-3362

Director of Admissions
Herron School of Art
1701 North Pennsylvania
Indianapolis, Indiana
46202
317-923-3651

Director of Admissions
Indiana State University
Terre Haute, Indiana
47809
812-232-6311

Director of Admissions
Indiana University
Bloomington, Indiana
47401
812-332-0211

Addresses (Cont.)

Director of Admissions
Purdue University
Executive Building
Lafayette, Indiana
47907
317-749-8111

Director of Admissions
Saint Mary's College
Notre Dame, Indiana

46556
219-232-3031

Director of Admissions
University of Evansville
P.O. Box 329
Evansville, Indiana
47701
812-479-2468

Additional Information

Executive Director
Indiana Arts Commission
15 East Washington Street
Indianapolis, Indiana
50319
515-281-5297

IOWA

Small *Coe College* has ceramics. Nothing else. *Cornell College* does a bit better; they have crafts and ceramics, all offered for nonmajors. *Northwestern College* has crafts, general and extremely limited. *Luther College* has a class in pottery. Period. *Southwestern Community College* has a couple of craft classes and one in mosaics. *Mount Mercy College* has some electives in ceramics. Nothing else.

Drake University has a BFA and MFA in silversmithing, jewelry. It also has a BFA in ceramics. The selection of crafts taught, however, is limited. Solid foundation stuff. *Grinnell College* has a BA in art, but crafts are limited to jewelry, ceramics and weaving. Crafts are not important at this school.

Iowa State University in Ames is much better; crafts are important here and it is one of the few places where you can get a BA and an MA in craft design. Most of the crafts are taught here. The *University of Iowa* has an excellent Art and Art History program and is well-equipped but leans toward the fine arts, though all crafts are taught, including quilting. Strong on theory, history and studio work. Big school. The *University of Northern Iowa* in Cedar Falls has both a BA and MA in plastics, jewelry and ceramics, but not a place that's highly regarded.

One very interesting summer place is *South Bear Creek School,* which features pottery, plus painting and poetry. Instruction is geared toward individual development. The small international faculty keeps close to the students. There are two potters at the place, which is in a large barn on the South Bear Creek in Highlandville, Iowa. Check it out. They sound like nice people. In Ames, The *Octagon* has courses in ceramics and weaving, year-round classes, mostly for beginners.

Addresses

Director of Admissions
Coe\College
Cedar Rapids, Iowa
52401
319-364-1511

Director of Admissions
Cornell College
Mount Vernon, Iowa
52314
319-895-8811

Director of Admissions
Drake University
Des Moines, Iowa
50311
515-271-2011

Director of Admissions
Grinnell College
Grinnell, Iowa
50112
515-236-6181

Director of Admissions
Iowa State University
Ames, Iowa
50010
515-294-4111

Director of Admissions
Luther College

Decorah, Iowa
52101
319-382-3621

Director of Admissions
Mount Mercy College
1330 Elmhurst Drive N.E.
Cedar Rapids, Iowa
52402
319-363-8213

Director of Admissions
Northwestern College
Orange City, Iowa
51041
712-737-4821

The Octagon
Ames Society for the Arts
232½ Main Street
Ames, Iowa
50010
515-232-4451

South Bear Creek School
c/o Dean L. Schwarz
Art Department
Luther College
Decorah, Iowa
52101
319-382-3621

Addresses (Cont.)

Director of Admissions
Southwestern Community College
Creston, Iowa
50801
515-782-7081

Director of Admissions
1 Jessup Hall
University of Iowa

Iowa City, Iowa
52240

Director of Admissions
University of Northern Iowa
Cedar Falls, Iowa
50613
219-273-2311

Additional Information

Executive Director
Iowa State Arts Council
State Capitol Building
Des Moines, Iowa
50319
515-281-5297

KANSAS

The little community college *Cloud County* has some general craft courses and also ceramics. That's it in their Art Department. Not worthwhile. *Fort Hays Kansas State College* does a lot better. It has a complete crafts curriculum with a BA and MA. Ceramics is particularly good. Darryl McGinnis teaches pottery. Excellent craftsman.

Friends University. Here's a top-notch place! A small campus of some 1,000 students and one of the more extensive crafts programs in the state. BFAs and MFAs granted. About one-third of all required course work is in a concentrated area, two-thirds are in the liberal arts section. A strong Quaker education is offered. Close community. Very fine college.

Kansas State College at Pittsburg also has BFA and MFA degrees. This school has a large faculty and a well-thought-out program. A foundation program is titled Visual Explorations, a series of four studio courses. Faculty works closely with the new students. Total curriculum is thirty-two craft courses, plus lectures in art history, education and appreciation. Lots of studio work, good equipment and buildings, good school.

Kansas State Teachers College trains, naturally, teachers. Their major programs are jewelry and ceramics. John Kudlacek is good here in pottery, but the school offers little else.

In Manhattan, Kansas, there's the large *Kansas State University.* You get almost any craft. The main programs are metal, ceramics, silversmithing. They grant BAs, BFAs, BSEs, but no graduate degrees. A particularly good teacher here is Angelo Garzio in pottery.

At *Marymount College,* a small co-ed Catholic liberal arts school, a few craft courses are offered: metals, ceramics, woodwork. Traditional place, nothing great. *Southwestern College* is a church-related school made up of five tiny colleges surrounding McPherson, Kansas. It has a very few craft classes: ceramics, general crafts. All beginning stuff.

The place to go to in Kansas is the *University of Kansas* at Lawrence. This college has it all. It offers a BFA in ceramics, design jewelry and silversmithing, and in textiles design. A common first-year program is given, then heavy concentration. Also an MA for art teachers. Outstanding professors here are Sheldon Carey (pottery), Eby DeGraw (weaving), Carlye Smith (metal).

Wichita State University has some crafts in the Art Department. They also offer tapestry, which is unusual. Ceramics is big and Richard St. John, who teaches pottery, is very fine indeed. Good place also for printmaking. At the *Wichita Art Association School* take Mary Snyder for weaving or Charles McDonald for silversmithing. Otherwise, avoid.

Addresses

Director of Admissions
Cloud County Community College
2221 Campus Drive
Concordia, Kansas
66901
913-243-1435

Director of Admissions
Fort Hays Kansas State College
Hays, Kansas
67601
913-628-4000

Director of Admissions
Friends University
2100 University
67203
316-263-9131

Director of Admissions
Kansas State College
Pittsburg, Kansas
66762
316-231-7000

Addresses (Cont.)

Director of Admissions
Kansas State Teachers College
Emporia, Kansas
66801
316-343-1200

Director of Admissions
Kansas State University
Manhattan, Kansas
66502
913-532-6011

Director of Admissions
Marymount College of Kansas
East Iron and Marymount Road
Salina, Kansas
67401
913-823-6317

Director of Admissions
Southwestern College
100 College

Winfield, Kansas
67156
316-221-4150

Director of Admissions
University of Kansas
Lawrence, Kansas
66044
913-864-3911

Director of Admissions
Wichita Art Association
9112 East Central
Wichita, Kansas
67206
316-683-9674

Director of Admissions
Wichita State University
1845 Fairmount
Wichita, Kansas
67208
316-689-3500

Additional Information

Executive Director
Kansas Cultural Arts Commission
120 North Oliver
Wichita, Kansas
67208
316-686-7411

KENTUCKY

The *University of Kentucky* has a BA and an MFA program. All students must take a set of required courses, called General Studies, standard college background courses. Majors are available in ceramics; that's all in crafts. There are weaving courses, design and some general crafts.

Western Kentucky University also has a BA and a BFA, no graduate work. Ceramics and weaving are the two craft areas. A wide range of classes, solid instruction, design courses also. Can study to be a teacher, elementary or secondary. It is difficult to understand the *University of Louisville*. It is difficult even to understand their catalog, big and impersonal as it is, but somewhere within the Fine Arts section they are offering ceramics, some jewelry, weaving and general craft courses. Department is tilted toward fine arts side of life. The college says, "Each person counts at the University." We doubt it. The school doesn't give that impression.

Asbury College is an independent liberal arts college in a "thoroughly Christian context." In their tiny Art Department they offer some ceramics courses. Nothing to write home about. *Morehead State University* has a few courses in ceramics, some general crafts. Classes are small and the department trains students for careers in "teaching, business and industry." Avoid.

Murray State University has classes in just about every craft, plus good three-dimensional design courses, and offers a BFA, or students can just major in one craft. A close faculty, the department helps students who want to continue studio work and/or go on to graduate school. Murray State has about 7,000 students and is located in a lovely town and lake area. We like this place.

The *Louisville School of Art* is the only four-year professional art school in the state of Kentucky and is an associate member of the National Association of Schools of Art. It offers a BFA in ceramics and crafts in general. The crafts offerings are many: wood, stone, foundry work, ceramics, textiles, metalsmithing, jewelry. This is a well-organized and worthy place.

Berea College is an old college, founded in 1855. It's for the students from 230 Appalachian counties. They take 80 percent of the 1,400 students from the area. Berea charges no tuition; expenses of board, room and incidentals for a year are about $1,000. You can study ceramics, weaving, metal and work in the school's handcrafted gift business that operates by catalog and a retail store. You learn a trade while earning expenses. Very fine place.

Campbellsville College is a school with a strong affiliation with the Kentucky Baptist Association. They offer a major in art with a teacher certification, a major in art with preparation for professional work or graduate school. The craft courses are ceramics, weaving, jewelry design. For the art education the courses cover crafts for school childern's work. Not much here.

Thomas More is a Catholic coeducational college that offers a BA in ceramics. The purpose of the Art Department is just to give a student a "sound grounding in studio and art history courses." Nothing offered in crafts beyond ceramics. *Kentucky Wesleyan College* in Owensboro does better. It has many more weaving and ceramics classes. There are also courses in jewelry and metalsmithing. A good department.

Addresses

Director of Admissions
Asbury College
Wilmore, Kentucky
40390
606-858-3511

Director of Admissions
Berea College
Berea, Kentucky
40403
606-986-3841

Director of Admissions
Campbellsville College
Campbellsville, Kentucky
42718
502-465-8158

Director of Admissions
Kentucky Wesleyan College
3000 Frederica Street
Owensboro, Kentucky
42301
502-684-5261

Louisville School of Art
100 Park Road
Anchorage, Kentucky
40223
502-245-8836

Director of Admissions
Morehead State University

Morehead, Kentucky
40351
606-783-2221

Director of Admissions
Murray State University
Murray, Kentucky
42071
502-762-3011

Director of Admissions
Thomas More College
P.O. Box 85
Covington, Kentucky
41017
606-341-5800

Director of Admissions
University of Kentucky
Lexington, Kentucky
40506
606-285-9000

Director of Admissions
University of Louisville
Louisville, Kentucky
40208
502-636-4101

Director of Admissions
Western Kentucky University
Bowling Green, Kentucky
42101
502-745-0111

Additional Information

Executive Director
Kentucky Arts Commisssion
Room 614, Capitol Plaza Tower
Frankfort, Kentucky
40601
502-564-3757

Kentucky Design Center
Route 3
Berea, Kentucky
40403
606-986-9806

LOUISIANA

Alternatives in New Orleans is one of the more exciting places to study in the state. Classes are in ceramics, stitchery, jewelry and weaving. Also lots of special classes. Very inexpensive place and friendly. Look them up. It's also a place where craftsmen gather. The *Weavers Workshop* is new and holds classes in beginning weaving, belt and card weaving, tapestry and rug weaving. They also give private lessons.

Louisiana State offers a BFA in glassblowing, ceramics and an MA in ceramics. John Bova and John Goodheart teach here, both very good teachers. Strong on ceramics. *Nicholls State University* has a small program; a BA is given in plastics and ceramics. Very straight. *Northeast Louisiana University* has a BA in crafts. They offer some general crafts, plus ceramics and weaving. Nothing much. *Tulane University* has some ceramics, nothing much here either. The *University of Southwestern Louisiana* has a strong ceramics department headed by Tom La Dusa. They offer a BA in ceramics and a BA in jewelry. That's all. And that is all for the state.

Addresses

Alternatives
714 Dublin Street
New Orleans, Louisiana
70115
504-866-6606

Director of Admissions
Louisiana State University
Baton Rouge, Louisiana
70806
504-388-3202

Director of Admissions
Nicholls State University
Thibodaux, Louisiana
70301
504-446-8111

Director of Admissions
Northeast Louisiana University
Monroe, Louisiana
71201
318-372-2100

Addresses (Cont.)

Director of Admissions
Tulane University
New Orelans, Louisiana
70118
504-865-4011

Director of Admissions
University of Southwestern
Louisiana

Lafayette, Louisiana
70501
318-233-3850

Weavers Workshop
1538 Danta Street
New Orleans, Louisiana
70118
504-866-0820

Additional Information

Executive Director
Louisiana Council of Arts
Suite 804, International Building
611 Gravier Street
New Orleans, Louisiana
70130
504-527-5070

MAINE

In this state you begin and end with *Haystack Mountain School of Crafts*. In 1950 it was established as a non-profit research and studio program and is famous for its summer program. Haystack is on Deer Isle, a rare and beautiful spot. Very hard to get accepted here, long waiting list. All the traditional crafts are taught.

Mandala is attempting to be a community arts and craft resource for the central Maine area. Drew Sanborn, the director, writes, "This means designing a program or programs that reach such diverse groups as the mill worker of French Canadian extraction, the sophisticated urban refugee, high school dropouts and middle-aged housewives." They offer ten-week course sessions in pottery, woodworking, jewelry, leather and weaving.

The *School of Fine and Applied Arts* is one of the oldest (and best) professional art schools in Maine. It has been mainly a school for professional painters, graphic and commercial artists. Now it offers a major in pottery and one in jewelry and silversmithing. All students take a foundation year, then concentrate. Intensive program and not expensive for what you receive. School is located in downtown Portland near the Museum of Art.

Home Co-op began as a low-income cooperative in rural Maine in 1970. Its purpose is to generate work for low-income and unemployed people who make hand-crafted products. It has been a grand success and now Home is building a craft village in Orland. They offer adult craft classes in most of the traditional crafts, open to all.

The *University of Maine* at Portland-Gorham has an art education degree with courses in ceramics, metal and weaving. Heavy on theory and art history, some independent craft studio work, but not much. Avoid unless you want to teach.

Addresses

Haystack Mountain School of Crafts
Deer Isle, Maine
04627
207-348-6946 (winter)
207-348-2816 (summer)

Home Co-op
Adult Education
Route 1
Orland, Maine
04472
207-469-3784

Mandala Community Workshop
4 North Street
Waterville, Maine

04901
207-872-7263

School of Fine and Applied Art
c/o Mr. William Collins
93 High Street
Portland, Maine
04101
207-775-3052

Director of Admissions
University of Maine at
Portland-Gorham
96 Falmouth Street
Portland, Maine
04103
207-773-2981

Additional Information

Executive Director
Maine State Commission on the Arts
State House
Augusta, Maine
04330
207-289-2724

MARYLAND

Just across the District of Columbia line on the Potomac Palisades is *Glen Echo Park*. Founded in 1891 at a Chautauqua assembly as "a natural citadel of culture on the banks of the Potomac," Glen Echo during the fifties and sixties was a large amusement park. The park closed in 1968 and was taken over by the National Park Service who with the support of the immediate community turned Glen Echo into a "Living Arts Center."

The coordinator of activities at Glen Echo is potter Wendy Ross, who has developed a series of experimental workshops, classes and demonstrations in crafts. The class offerings in the past have been weaving, spinning, silvercasting, pottery, enameling, stained glass and jewelry.

The first two summers of full-time operation suffered some from poor planning and lack of funds, but the Park is gradually moving toward year-round operation. Already a potter has classes throughout the year. This is another example of the National Parks Service working with local people in developing craft centers. There is one immediate problem, however. Glen Echo needs money and some long-range planning to change the atmosphere from that of a penny arcade to an arts center.

Also close to Washington, D.C., is the two-year community college of *Montgomery*. Within its Department of Visual Communications Technologies is a full year of ceramics and printmaking, also a semester course in weaving and a semester of jewelry making. The college has two campuses, but all crafts are located in Rockland. Montgomery College offers good introductory work and the Art Department has enough design and theory courses to give good fundamentals, but the college is not a great place to attend. There are no engaging campuses or lifestyles, but the Rockville campus does have its own self-contained art building, which is a beaut!

Also near D.C. is huge *University of Maryland* at College Park. Here within the Department of Housing and Applied Design is their craft offering, a four-year crafts curriculum leading to a major. Maryland University is expanding its craft offerings, but the department curriculum is still heavy with "typical" courses leading to a liberal arts degree. It is only in the upper division, mainly the senior year, where most of the student's time is devoted to crafts, and here there is solid concentration. The University of Maryland does have the resources and the equipment, if one can handle the huge and unattractive campus.

On the banks of the St. Mary's River is a small (850 students) coeducational four-year state liberal arts college called, not surprisingly, *St. Mary's College of Maryland*. Recently it designed a new humanities program with a major emphasis on art and crafts. The program has three basic art experiences: a study of theories underlying art; a study of content in courses which essentially take the form of art history, focusing on the study of artists and artifacts in a classroom setting; and finally, an exploration of studio principles ranging from basic techniques to the creation of art in a variety of visual art media. This is a well-balanced program and St. Mary's has good studio space and new equipment, including two glass furnaces. The crafts now being taught are ceramics, jewelry, silversmithing, weaving, glassblowing, pottery and woodworking.

Within Baltimore there's the very fine *Maryland Institute, College of Art,* a non-profit, private school that is a member of the Union of Independent Colleges of Art. There are majors here offered in all aspects of art, including a designer-craftsman program. The college awards BFAs, diplomas and graduate masters.

The Maryland Institute is in downtown Baltimore on Bolton Hill housed in seven buildings that are mixed into an old residential area now being renovated. This is an old school, first chartered in 1826. All students are required to take a one-year foundation program of Western art and ideas, plus English and basic art skills. The Maryland Institute is a traditional and highly organized place with grades and attendance requirements. Keep that in mind when applying.

Also in Baltimore is the *College of Notre Dame of Maryland*. This is a Catholic and traditional four-year place. It does, however, have some innovative programs, such as a 4-1-4 calendar and they are part of an inter-institutional exchange program. Within the Art Department are courses in ceramics, sculpture (welding) and some general printing and craft survey courses, but not much beyond beginning lessons. The college at times calls itself "homey" and that pretty much is what it is.

The *Community College of Baltimore* is not an impressive place, but a beginning crafts person can pick up a few courses in ceramics, drawing and design, printmaking. Most of the Art Department is geared toward commercial art. A student can do a lot better in the Baltimore area, but the classes here are inexpensive, if elementary and artsy-craftsy.

The *Baltimore Museum of Art* offers a limited set of craft courses, mainly for beginners. They have classes in ceramics, sculpture in wood, graphics (woodcut and intaglio), and there are drawing and painting classes as well. These courses are concerned with the esthetics of the craft and are offered for one day a week. There are two twelve-week terms, one in the fall and one in the spring, as well as a four-week term in the summer. Not really for a person serious about crafts.

Near Baltimore is *Towson State College*. It's a new four-year college teaching crafts. The program is limited at the moment. There are courses in enameling, jewelry, ceramics, wood and weaving. All beginning stuff. The *Weaver's Place* has classes in all areas of weaving. Some special courses are: Theo Moorman Tapestry Techniques, inkle weaving, drawdown, dyeing (chemical and natural). All good people here.

Addresses

Baltimore Museum of Art
Art Museum Drive
Baltimore, Maryland
21218
301-889-1735

Director of Admissions
College of Notre Dame of
Maryland
4701 North Charles Street
Baltimore, Maryland
21210
301-435-0100

Director of Admissions
Community College of Baltimore

2901 Liberty Heights Avenue
Baltimore, Maryland
21215
301-462-5800

Director of Admissions
Maryland Institute, College of Art
1300 Mount Royal Avenue
Baltimore, Maryland
21217
301-669-9200

Director of Admissions
Montgomery College
51 Mannakee Street

Rockville, Maryland
20850
301-762-7400

Glen Echo Park
National Park Service
Glen Echo, Maryland
20768
301-229-3031

Director of Admissions
St. Mary's College of Maryland
St. Mary's City, Maryland
20686
301-994-1600

Director of Admissions
Towson State College

Baltimore, Maryland
21204
301-823-7500

Director of Admissions
University of Maryland
College Park, Maryland
20742
301-454-2135

Weaver's Place
2137 Gwynn Oak Avenue
Baltimore, Maryland
21207
301-265-6544

Individual Instruction

CERAMICS

Charles Tester
9921 Rhode Island Avenue
College Park, Maryland
20740
301-441-2863

MACRAMÉ

Mrs. Seymour Bress
4806 Camelot Street
Rockville, Maryland
20853
301-881-4770

WEAVING

Mrs. Allan S. Arness
3915 Washington Street
Kensington, Maryland
20795
301-949-0031

P. Hendley Napier
412 Southwest Drive
Silver Spring, Maryland
20901
301-593-6070

Mrs. Walter E. Pocock
1225 Elm Ridge Avenue
Baltimore, Maryland
21229
301-242-6453

Mrs. Luc Secretan
5906 Mustang Drive
Riverdale, Maryland
20840
301-927-1232

Mrs. Richard J. Vernon
3718 Ramsgate Drive
Annapolis, Maryland
21403
301-269-0288

Mary Judik Wise
Glenarm Road
Glen Arm, Maryland
21057
301-668-6365

WEAVING, MACRAMÉ

Mrs. Lowell W. Bennett
16801 Redland Road
Derwood, Maryland
20855
301-762-6794

Individual Instruction (Cont.)

WEAVING, QUILTING

Mrs. K. H. Miller
4604 S. Chelsea Lane
Bethesda, Maryland
20014
301-657-3853

Additional Information

Executive Director
Maryland Arts Council
15 West Mulberry
Baltimore, Maryland
21210
301-685-7470

MASSACHUSETTS

This state is alive with craft opportunities, especially in the Boston area. We've tried to find the more interesting places to learn a skill, schools and studios where a person can work exclusively (or nearly exclusively) in crafts.

There's a viable non-profit corporation called *Mudflat* that enrolls about one hundred students at a time with classes limited to only ten students. There are beginning, intermediate and advanced courses in pottery. The average course is twelve lessons of three hours each, meeting twice a week. The classes are inexpensive, no cost for practice, and the studio is open seven days a week. There are also special classes in glaze application, kiln construction and operation, and handbuilding techniques.

A small place to learn glasswork is the *Stained Glass Workshop* in Boston. It's run by Ann and Henry Adams, both graduates of Harvard, who taught glasswork in San Francisco before moving back to Boston. Henry originally learned stained glass in 1970 when he worked with German craftsmen in Milwaukee. Their basic class aims at teaching techniques and the advanced class covers, among other things, color theory.

The outline of the basic class is: "You will design and make a leaded glass window about a square foot in size. In doing so, you will learn the basic techniques of stained glass including designing, cutting glass, leading, soldering, cementing and finishing. The class includes a slide discussion illustrating the history of stained glass."

Classes here are inexpensive, about $25 for six weeks. When not teaching Ann and Henry do research on the nineteenth-century stained glass designer John LaFarge.

Craft Center is a very fine place indeed! It was first started in 1951 as a "non-profit educational institution dedicated to the promotion of education in the crafts." It has outstanding classes in woodworking, ceramics, metalwork, enameling, weaving and design/printmaking. The classes are scheduled once a week for three hours. A course runs for ten weeks. The instruction is first class and in great detail. For example, enameling: "Enameling on copper is a course designed to acquaint students with twenty basic techniques as well as cloisonné, Grisaille, Basse Taille and Limoges."

Another non-profit organization is *Project, Inc.* This is an art, photography and ceramics workshop center. The emphasis at Project is on small group classes "providing the students with maximum individualized attention."

Project was organized by a group of parents to "help supplement their children's education in the visual arts." It has now expanded to teach courses for adults. The school has a large and well-experienced teaching staff, especially in ceramics. Courses in batik and tie-dye, fibers and jewelry are limited, but there are nine or more offerings in ceramics.

The Boston YWCA has the *Workshop* with contemporary crafts classes for everybody. Courses are "planned for every kind of individual—those who want an intensive participation in the program or a weekend experience." The studios here are among the best in Boston. Classes are available in almost everything: jewelry, enameling, weaving, batik, ceramics. The ceramics studio is on the eighth floor, off in a spacious corner with both light and view. Students can use the studio before and after class. Terms last from ten to twelve weeks, usually meeting once a week for several hours. Costs vary but are reasonable.

In Lincoln the *Decordova Museum School of Art* has a particularly good museum crafts program with classes in almost all areas. There is a large but only adequate faculty. All teach part-time. Start here when you're beginning, even if they are structured and straight. Foundation work well-taught.

Now, the *School of the Museum of Fine Arts* in Boston is something else. It's accredited by the National Association of Schools of Art, offers a BFA in conjunction with Tufts University, also has a masters program. There are about 490 students, all full-time, and a faculty of over forty. This is a very open school. They advise students, "It could very well be that the Boston Museum School is the wrong school for you—especially if you feel that you need a highly structured and disciplined first year foundation program . . ." To obtain a degree you'll have to take non-craft courses, but the diploma program is offered for those who want just studio work. Ceramics, jewelry and metalsmithing are the main craft areas.

Also in Boston is the *Massachusetts College of Art,* one hundred years old. It's unique as the only publicly supported institution of higher education in the arts. They have about 1,000 students and are growing rapidly. Mass Art offers BFAs in art education, design and fine arts.

The purpose of the craft department is "to introduce the craft techniques of clay, metal and textile to students interested in the crafts and to allow continued study and development over a three-year period." Students are prepared to teach crafts in schools. That's the way they figure crafts are useful. Mostly an arts college, but first-rate.

At the following schools you can "be in college" and study crafts. The program at *Southeastern Massachusetts University* has an Art Teacher Education major that takes into account craft courses. *Regis College,* the women's college in Weston, has a few ceramics offerings in their art program.

At the huge campus of the *University of Massachusetts* at Amherst there is a very highly developed art curriculum where one can study ceramics, but not much else in crafts. The BFA program has "greater latitude of core requirements" and you'll learn a lot about art history. *Endicott Junior College* in Beverly has minor offerings in ceramics and some general education stuff.

Some other places to get started in crafts are the *Cambridge Center for Adult Education* and the *Boston Center for Adult Education*. Both have inexpensive courses in a wide range of crafts. These centers are private and non-profit and were established "to reinforce the idea that education is a life-long process." Take advantage of them; they're worth it.

In the historic town of Nantucket on Nantucket Island is the *Nantucket School of Needlery*. This school is sponsored by the Nantucket Historical Trust, which brings needlework authorities from all over the world to teach and train at the school. The Nantucket School also has a home study course. It's very fine.

Addresses

Boston Center for Adult
Education
5 Commonwealth Avenue
Boston, Massachusetts
02116
617-267-4430

Cambridge Center for Adult
Education
42 Brattle Street
Cambridge, Massachusetts
02138
617-547-6789

Craft Center
25 Sagamore Road
Worcester, Massachusetts
01605
617-753-8183

Decordova Museum School of Art
Lincoln, Massachusetts
01773
617-259-8355

Director of Admissions
Endicott Junior College
Beverly, Massachusetts
01915
617-927-0585

Massachusetts College of Art
364 Brookline Avenue
Boston, Massachusetts
02215
617-731-2340

Mudflat
196 Broadway
Cambridge, Massachusetts
02139
617-354-9626

Nantucket School of Needlery
2 India Street
Nantucket Island
Massachusetts
02554
617-228-1909

Project, Inc.
141 Huron Avenue
Cambridge, Massachusetts
02138
617-491-0187

Director of Admissions
Regis College
Weston, Massachusetts
02193
617-893-1820

Addresses (Cont.)

School of the Museum of Fine Art
230 The Fenway
Boston, Massachusetts
02115
617-267-9300

Director of Admissions
Southeastern Massachusetts
University
North Dartmouth, Massachusetts
02747
617-997-9321

The Stained Glass Workshop
23 Tavern Road

Boston, Massachusetts
02115
617-442-9464

Director of Admissions
University of Massachusetts
Amherst, Massachusetts
01002
413-545-0111

The Workshop
Boston YWCA
140 Clarendon Street
Boston, Massachusetts
02116
617-536-7940

Additional Information

Massachusetts Council on the Arts
14 Beacon Street
Boston, Massachusetts
02108
617-727-3668

MEXICO

The place I'd recommend for schooling in Mexico is *Instituto Allende*. This is Latin America's oldest and largest school of arts, crafts, writing and language for English-speaking students. It is incorporated with the University of Guanajuato and is an accredited member of the Asociación Nacional de Universidades. They have a School of Design and Crafts and the major crafts are textiles, metal and ceramics. There are also courses in jewelry, glassblowing, welding and forging. This school is well-equipped and has a fine faculty. It is possible to study here and transfer credits back to the US colleges.

Address

Executive Director
Instituto Allende
San Miguel de Allende, Gto.
Mexico

MICHIGAN

This state has many colleges offering craft courses, but not many with studios or private teaching. One private place, however, is with *Ruth Scherer*. She teaches spinning and weaving in Trout Lake; that's in the Upper Peninsula. She writes, "I offer three basic 5-day courses, one spinning; two backstrap loom weaving; three floor loom weaving. The work is all on an individual basis with each student, although I do take up to five students at a time in the same course. Class work is from 9 A.M. to 4 P.M. Students stay in the village nearby. I do have students coming for critique and for any desired special work that they wish."

The *Birmingham Art Center* has the purpose of providing "a community-wide, integrated studio-gallery center." Four semesters of classes are held during the year, mornings, afternoons, evenings. The crafts offered are in ceramics, jewelry and loom weaving. There's also advanced fiber classes. This is an active center, but again only for beginners.

Kalamazoo Institute of Arts has a small school that offers classes in ceramics, jewelry and weaving taught by teachers from the local colleges. Instruction is at all levels. A very good place. Highly recommended. The *Flint Institute of Arts* in the De Waters Art Center gives a couple of courses in ceramics, a beginning weaving class. Not much.

Among colleges *Alma* has an Art Department that deals with crafts but in a limited way. Craft courses are general. Not a place for a serious student. However the *Art School of the Society of Arts and Crafts* in Detroit is a very good school. It's accredited by the National Association of Schools of Art, for people who worry about such things, and awards a BFA in ceramics, metal and jewelry among others. There you can also take weaving and fabric design, wood and glass. Almost all the student's time is spent in studio work, except for the BFA students who take classes in English, art history, philosophy and psychology. This school is a non-profit place, well-equipped and well worth the money.

Big and impersonal *Eastern Michigan University* offers a BFA and teaches just about everything in crafts. Ceramics and jewelry are the big areas. Solid foundation work, but not much imagination here. Good studio space. What you'd expect from a state college.

There are some two-year community colleges offering crafts. *Genesee Community College* has a couple of classes, nothing much: ceramics, metalsmithing and jewelry, also art history. Avoid the place. *Henry Ford College* offers very little in crafts, some ceramics, art appreciation. Again avoid.

Hillsdale College is a small four-year school, under 1,500 students. A straight place. A nice place. Their craft offerings are mostly foundation work. Ceramics, jewelry are offered. All courses in the Art Department and fine arts dominates.

Michigan State University offers all sorts of degrees, BFAs, MFAs. The major areas are ceramics and jewelry. Lots of requirements and prerequisites. Grades are important here. You can earn a teaching degree. I'd avoid State. Connected with State is the Mary Chase Perry museum in Detroit. It's called *Pewabic Pottery*. (Mary Chase Perry, later Stratton, was a glaze chemist who discovered the Iridescent and Egyptian Blue glazes.) Adult classes are taught here in pottery all year round by Michigan State faculty. A tremendous number of people apply, so they use a lottery system, picking only local applicants. They have plans to expand to 150 students per term, now take about 60.

Up north in Marquette, *Northern Michigan University* trains teachers in their Visual Arts Department. They have courses in ceramics, metal, wood, weaving and also furniture design, one of the few places for this in the state. Nothing very exciting up here.

The huge *University of Michigan* in its College of Architecture and Design has a Department of Art. This is a very professional place. A student would do well to go here. Unfortunately, ceramics is all that's offered in crafts. They award BFAs and MFAs. Difficult to be accepted here; they like students with some experience and developed skills. Take a lot of upper division transfer students.

Western Michigan University in Kalamazoo offers BFAs and MFAs. The craft opportunities here are in many areas, but ceramics, jewelry and textile design are major areas. A solid academic place, not very inventive however. Requirements and special tests must be passed. A large faculty.

But when you talk about crafts schools in Michigan—or talk about craft schools in America—you talk about *Cranbrook Academy of Art.* Cranbrook "began informally with a group of artists and craftsmen assembled in 1927 by Mr. and Mrs. George Gough Booth." It was to be "a community of creative people, a learning environment where artist-instructors and students work, communicate and grow together."

You can earn a BFA, an MFA, anything you want here. But it's hard getting into Cranbrook as an undergraduate. They say, "The Academy offers—to a limited number of exceptionally prepared candidates—the undergraduate degree in eight of its nine fields, the exception being architecture."

The programs are in ceramics, design, fabrics, metalsmithing, painting, photography, printmaking and sculpture and architecture. Cranbrook has many of the best crafts teachers in the world, either full-time or visiting. Just can't do better. A lovely campus of 300 acres of woods and lakes. Close to Detroit. New equipment and building. Everything!

Addresses

Director of Admissions
Alma College
Superior Street
Alma, Michigan
48880
517-463-2141

Registrar
Art School of the Society of Arts
and Crafts

245 East Kirby
Detroit, Michigan
48202
313-872-3118

Ruth M. Scherer Studio
Birch Shores
Trout Lake, Michigan
49793
906-569-3237

Addresses (Cont.)

Bloomfield Art Association
1516 South Cranbrook Road
Birmingham, Michigan
48009
313-644-0866

Director of Admissions
Cranbrook Academy of Art
Box 806
Bloomfield Hills, Michigan
48013
313-644-1600

Director of Admissions
Eastern Michigan University
Ypsilanti, Michigan
48197
313-487-1849

Flint Institute of Arts
1120 East Kearsley Street
Flint, Michigan
48503
313-234-1695

Director of Admissions
Genesee Community College
1401 East Court Street
Flint, Michigan
48503
313-238-1631

Director of Admissions
Henry Ford College
5101 Evergreen Road
Dearborn, Michigan
48128
313-271-2750

Director of Admissions
Hillsdale College

Hillsdale, Michigan
49242
517-437-7341

Kalamazoo Institute of Arts
314 South Park Street
Kalamazoo, Michigan
49006
616-349-7775

Director of Admissions
Michigan State University
East Lansing, Michigan
48823
517-355-8330

Roger Audt
MSU/Pewabic Pottery
10125 East Jefferson
Detroit, Michigan
48214
313-822-0954

Director of Admissions
Northern Michigan University
Marquette, Michigan
49855
906-227-1000

Director of Admissions
University of Michigan
1220 Student Activities Building
Ann Arbor, Michigan
48104
313-764-7433

Director of Admissions
Western Michigan University
Kalamazoo, Michigan
49001
616-383-1600

Individual Instruction

FIBER CRAFTS
Anita E. Meyland
606 Pine Street
Marquette, Michigan
49855

WEAVING
Nadine Janke
405 Huron Street
Houghton, Michigan
49931

WOODCARVING
Pat and Niron Virch
1506 Lynn Avenue
Marquette, Michigan
49855

Additional Information

Paul Wilson
Upper Peninsula Crafts Council
Box 246 A, Route 1
Sault Ste. Marie, Michigan
49783

Executive Director
Michigan Council for the Arts
10125 East Jefferson Avenue
Detroit, Michigan
48214
313-222-1091

MINNESOTA

Gail's Ceramic Studio has instruction in wheel, coil, slab methods for functional, non-functional and sculpture ceramic stoneware. Instruction also in the use of high fire glazes for ceramic stoneware. Students attend one three-hour class session per week. Personal instruction. The *Minnesota Museum Art School* has pottery, jewelry and weaving. Beginner's work. The *Rochester Art Center* is a bit better, slightly wider selection of courses, but no advance work.

Bemidji State College is a small college in the northern part of the state. It has a Department of Art and it trains treachers. Some ceramics and jewelry. There isn't much to work with here. *Mankato State College* has a lot to offer a crafts person: a BFA and an MFA, a large faculty and all crafts are taught in depth. Very fine place! It has a large campus, about 12,000 students. But it's cold up here in the North.

Little *St. Cloud State College,* although a lovely campus in a lovely town, has about six craft possibilities, all leading nowhere. They are tied into the Art Department.

Carleton College is simply a first-rate college in every sense. The problem, however, is that they lack an extensive crafts program. The college is very academic and it's hard for them to admit the value of studio work. Carleton has ceramics and some metal work. The place is outstanding for the fine arts and history of art. Small faculty.

St. Paul's *College of St. Catherine,* a straight Catholic women's college, has some crafts—pottery, jewelry, wood and welded sculpture—but this place trains teachers. Little serious professional work. *St. Mary's Junior College* in Minneapolis is another Catholic school. This has a couple of craft courses, but nothing worthwhile.

The *University of Minnesota* at *Duluth* and *Minneapolis* has sizeable craft programs. At Minneapolis you can earn a BFA and MFA in glass, glassblowing, metal and ceramics. Duluth is more limited and has only a BA, yet it has a wider selection of crafts offered. Of the two, Minneapolis is better, if you like big state colleges and campuses.

Addresses

Director of Admissions
Bemidji State College
Bemidji, Minnesota
56601
218-755-2000

Director of Admissions
Carleton College
Northfield, Minnesota
55057
507-645-4431

Director of Admissions
The College of St. Catherine
2004 Randolph Avenue
St. Paul, Minnesota
55105
612-698-5571

Gail Kristensen
Gail's Ceramic Studio
1775 Hillcrest
St. Paul, Minnesota
55116
612-698-9516

Director of Admissions
Mankato State College
Mankato, Minnesota
56001
507-389-1823

Rochester Art Center
Mayo Park
Rochester, Minnesota
55901
507-282-8629

Minnesota Museum Art School
30 East 10th Street
St. Paul, Minnesota
55101
612-227-7613

Director of Admissions
St. Cloud State College
St. Cloud, Minnesota
56301
612-255-0121

Director of Admissions
St. Mary's Junior College
2600 South Sixth Street

Minneapolis, Minnesota
55406
612-332-5521

Director of Admissions
University of Minnesota
Duluth, Minnesota
55812
218-726-7507

Director of Admissions
University of Minnesota
Minneapolis, Minnesota
55455
612-373-2851

Additional Information

Executive Director
Minnesota State Arts Council
100 East 22nd Street
Minneapolis, Minnesota
55404
612-296-2059

MISSISSIPPI

Mississippi State College for Women has a large art department in its own huge building, plus an annex, and an adequate selection of craft courses. You can take acrylic painting, pottery, jewelry, printmaking, plus design classes. Most of the teaching is traditional and they offer, for example, a course on origins of contemporary art that stops at 1913. The campus is on a hundred acres in downtown Columbus, a lovely southern place. That's about all it has going for it.

William Carey College has even less to offer. They have three semester hours of something called "creative crafts" and three hours only of ceramics. The aim of the Art Department is "to help the student develop a means of self-expression and to encourage and promote creativity in all aspects of life." The school does have some design and art history, that's about all.

At *Delta State College* the Art Department trains teachers for elementary and secondary schools. They do, however, have a good selection of courses in crafts: ceramics, metals, tie-dye, woodcarving. Very highly structured though. Don't expect much and you won't be disappointed.

The *University of Mississippi* has both a BFA and an MFA, but the crafts person will find only ceramics here, and then highly structured and only in the junior and senior years. But you can major in ceramics and that's something!

Addresses

Director of Admissions
Delta State College
Cleveland, Mississsippi
38732
601-843-9441

Director of Admissions
Mississippi State College for
Women
Box 70
Columbus, Mississippi
39701
601-328-5891

Director of Admissions
University of Mississippi
University, Mississippi
38677
601-232-5945

Director of Admissions
William Carey College
Hattiesburg, Mississippi
39401
601-582-5051

Additional Information

Executive Director
Mississippi Arts Commission
State Executive Building
P.O. Box 1341
Jackson, Mississippi
39205
601-354-7336

MISSOURI

Avila College is a small Catholic coeducational school. It offers some ceramics classes in the Art Department. This place lacks a lot of imagination, a straight place. *Central Missouri State*

College is another Missouri school with little to offer, only general ceramics in the Art Department.

The *Craft Alliance Center* is a "not for profit organization" that offers courses in ceramics and textiles. Classes are offered throughout the year. The Alliance is made up of about forty-five craftsmen. The staff changes with each session.

The *Kansas City Art Institute* has a BFA in ceramics and also offers almost all other crafts. It's a charter member of the National Association of Schools of Art. It's an old school (1885) and a fine school. Interviews are held for all applicants. The school is south of the city in Kansas City and housing is possible for 180 students. Other students live in town. They have about 250 students. This is one of the best craft schools in the Midwest.

Lincoln University is not an exciting place. They train art teachers. Small staff. Nothing much here for a serious crafts person. *Northeast Missouri State University* has a Division of Fine Arts and prepares teachers also. Courses in ceramics, weaving. Some sculpture.

Northwest Missouri State University has more to offer, a BFA in ceramics, jewelry, metalsmithing and design. The school also has a major in art-psychology, an unusual combination. This is for students in art therapy. The Art Department is large, many classes in crafts, a large staff. Recommended.

Southeast Missouri State College is located in the lovely town of Cape Girardeau. A college that has craft courses in almost all areas, but no BFA. Small faculty that gives a good foundation work. At *Southwest Missouri State College* in Springfield there's a BFA in ceramics, metal-jewelry and weaving. Also possible to take a large segment of individual craft study. A craft place worth considering.

Stephens College is a women's school in Columbia, Missouri, with an enrollment of 2,000. Columbia is a college town, and not much of a town. The college is strong in art, a BFA is offered. Ceramics, stained glass and design classes possible. But not a crafts place. No one is serious here.

The large system of the *University of Missouri* has several campuses, but only the *Columbia* and *St. Louis* campuses matter. They have BA and MA degrees, offer general crafts, jewelry, ceramics and weaving, but none of this is really that valuable. You can do better elsewhere in the state. The masters program is more worthwhile, a high concentration on crafts there.

Washington University has one of the truly fine arts colleges in the Midwest. The school offers a BFA and an MFA in metal and ceramics. Located on a large and beautiful campus, this is a residential place. A tough, traditional and well-worthwhile school. The studio work is extensive and the atmosphere open.

William Woods College has a degree program in art, has some classes in jewelry and ceramics. Not much else. Not much either at *Florissant Valley Community College* in St. Louis. Some courses in ceramics, design.

Addresses

Director of Admissions
Avila College
11901 Wornall Road
Kansas City, Missouri
64145
816-942-3204

Director of Admissions
Central Missouri State College
Warrensburg, Missouri
64093
816-747-9145

Craft Alliance Center
6640 Delmer
St. Louis, Missouri
63130
314-725-1177

Director of Admissions
Florissant Valley Community
College
3400 Pershall Road
St. Louis, Missouri
63135
314-524-2020

Kansas City Art Institute
4415 Warwick Boulevard

Kansas City, Missouri
64111
816-561-4852

Director of Admissions
Lincoln University of Missouri
Jefferson City, Missouri
65101
314-751-2325

Director of Admissions
Northeast Missouri State
University
Kirksville, Missouri
63501
816-665-5121

Director of Admissions
Northwest Missouri State
University
De Luce Fine Arts Building
Maryville, Missouri
64468
816-582-4669

Director of Admissions
Southeast Missouri State College
Cape Girardeau, Missouri
63701
314-334-8211

Director of Admissions
Southwest Missouri State College
Springfield, Missouri
65802
417-831-1561

Director of Admissions
Stephens College
Columbia, Missouri
65201
314-442-2211

Director of Admissions
University of Misssouri
Jesse Hall
Columbia, Missouri
65201
314-882-2121

Director of Admissions
University of Missouri
8001 Natural Bridge Road
St. Louis, Missouri
63121
314-453-0111

Director of Admissions
Washington University
202 Bixby Hall
St. Louis, Missouri
63130
314-863-0100

Director of Admissions
William Woods College
Fulton, Missouri
65251
314-642-2251

Additional Information

Executive Director
Missouri State Council on the Arts
Suite 410
111 South Bemiston
St. Louis, Missouri
63105
314-721-1672

MONTANA

The *Archie Bray Foundation* established in 1951 by three friends teaches glassblowing, one of the few such places in the country, and also has an extensive ceramics program. It was established "to make available for all who are seriously and sincerely interested in any of the branches of the ceramic art." It is, as they say, "a fine place to work." Check it out.

At the *College of Great Falls* the Art Department has lots of requirements, but few craft courses. Ceramics is offered, as are silversmithing and jewelry, some general stuff. You can do better elsewhere in this state. Great Falls is a Catholic college, independent, and for men and women.

Eastern Montana College has courses in crafts, among them ceramics, metal work, jewelry. The college is in Billings, an ideal college town. It is one of the better schools for crafts in Montana. We recommend it. No BFA, however.

Two community colleges, *Miles* and *Flathead Valley,* have craft courses. Miles is real beginner's stuff, but Flathead Valley offers design and ceramics at all levels. Best of the two places. *Western Montana College* offers only general crafts and ceramics. About twelve hours all together. They've established the art program for secondary art teachers. Not much here.

The *University of Montana* is offering a BFA, MA and an MFA. They have an outstanding ceramics program under the direction of Rudy Autio. The Design/Crafts Program is directed by Maxine Blackmer. They offer studio work in textile decoration, small metal work, enameling, jewelry-fabrication and casting, some lapidary and individual work in current trends. Soon they'll have an electroforming area. Throughout the year they have workshops by "name" artists in ceramics. Highly recommended.

Northern Montana College has little to offer, a few ceramics courses and they are hardly worth mentioning. *Rocky Mountain College* has a major in art, but craft courses are limited to some ceramics, jewelry and craft courses in general. A bad college, however.

Addresses

Archie Bray Foundation
2915 Country Club Avenue
Helena, Montana
59601
406-442-2521

Director of Admissions
College of Great Falls
1301 20th Street South
Great Falls, Montana
59405
406-761-8210

Director of Admissions
Eastern Montana College
Billings, Montana
59101
406-657-2011

Director of Admissions
Flathead Valley Community
P.O. Box 1174
Kalispell, Montana
59901
406-752-3411

Director of Admissions
Miles Community College
2715 Dickenson Street
Miles City, Montana
59301
406-232-3031

Director of Admissions
Northern Montana College
Havre, Montana
59501
406-265-7821

Director of Admissions
Rocky Mountain College

Billings, Montana
59102
406-245-6151

Director of Admissions
University of Montana
Missoula, Montana
59801
406-243-0211

Director of Admissions
Western Montana College
Dillon, Montana
59725
406-683-7011

Additional Information

Executive Director
Montana Arts Council
Fine Arts Building
University of Montana
59801
406-243-4883

NEBRASKA

Crafts at *Chadron State College* is limited to ceramics, glass-blowing, some metal work and advanced work in ceramics. All three-dimensional courses are taught by one professor. The Division of Fine Arts has many requirements and programs that students must fit into, but the craft courses themselves are complete and worthy. But you're only getting one man's ideas and techniques.

Peru State College is just a little school with some ceramics courses in their Art Department, about three hours total. Nothing here.

At the *University of Nebraska at Lincoln* they offer a BFA, a "well-rounded" education. There are courses in everything besides art or crafts that students must take. Actually there aren't many craft courses; some ceramics, jewelry, design theory, that's all. You can do better elsewhere in the state.

The *University of Nebraska at Omaha* has a BFA degree but their crafts are limited to ceramics and it is really a fine arts degree that you're getting. Not much.

Two other possibilities are: *Haymarket Gallery* in Lincoln, which has courses in batik, jewelry, weaving. Small classes, but mostly hobby level. *Joselyn Art Museum* has courses in jewelry and needleweaving. Also hobby level.

Addresses

Director of Admissions
Chadron State College
810 Moorehead
Chadron, Nebraska
69337
308-432-5571

Haymarket Art Gallery
119 South 9th
Lincoln, Nebraska
68508
402-432-7373

Joselyn Art Museum
2200 Dodge Street
Omaha, Nebraska
68102
402-342-3996

Director of Admissions
Peru State College

1117 Fifth Street
Peru, Nebraska
68421
402-872-3815

Director of Admissions
University of Nebraska at Lincoln
109 Administration Building
Lincoln, Nebraska
68508
402-472-7211

Director of Admissions
University of Nebraska at Omaha
Box 688 Downtown Station
Omaha, Nebraska
68132
402-553-4700

Individual Instruction

WEAVING

Mrs. Cornelin W. Nelson
2222 South 15 Street
Omaha, Nebraska
68108

Additional Information

Executive Secretary
Nebraska Arts Council
P.O. Box 1536
Omaha, Nebraska
68101
402-345-2542

NEVADA

At the *University of Nevada at Las Vegas* it's possible to earn a BFA; this is a good place to study. The art program is broad, you can study ceramics, metal, plastics. All design courses in three dimensions. The department "encourages individual exploration and creativity." The school is good on fundamentals and wants students to learn all the techniques.

In *Reno* at the *University of Nevada* a lot less is offered. Some courses are given in jewelry, ceramics and stitchery. Not much. Go to Las Vegas.

Addresses

Director of Admissions
University of Nevada at Las Vegas
Las Vegas, Nevada
89109
702-784-6866

Director of Admissions
University of Nevada at Reno
Reno, Nevada
89507
702-739-3671

Additional Information

Executive Secretary
Nevada State Council on the Arts
P.O. Box 1536
Omaha, Nebraska
68101
402-345-2542

NEW HAMPSHIRE

Sharon Arts Center is an incorporated non-profit organization devoted to the "teaching, promotion, and appreciation of arts and crafts." It is affiliated with the New Hampshire League of Craftsmen. Located five miles south of Peterborough, it offers a year-round program of classes, exhibitions and lectures. It was started in 1947 by William and Ruth Young as a place for people in the Monadnock region to study crafts. The center now offers courses in pottery, weaving, jewelry making, metalwork and enameling. This is a good place, with students—as well as teachers and lecturers—from all over the United States.

The *Arts and Science Center* is the community center for Nashua, a friendly and folksy place. The craft courses they offer are handbuilt pottery, batik, designing with stained glass. This isn't a serious place to learn crafts, not when they also offer classes in cake decorating. In the Nashua area and for beginners, it's fine.

Another small non-profit community center is the *Manchester Institute of Arts.* They offer craft courses in jewelry and silversmithing, weaving, ceramics and stitchery, which are given on all levels. Very active place, but for beginners.

There is also not much in New Hampshire among colleges. *Colby College* is a women's junior college of 600 students that has within its arts curriculum a couple of semesters of ceramics, that's all! They also have classes in the appreciation of art and fine arts, but this college isn't for a student serious about crafts.

The little Catholic women's college, *Notre Dame,* has a small Art Department and some classes in crafts. They teach ceramics, beginning and advanced. They do have aesthetic and appreciation classes, fundamental stuff, but you can't go very far in any one craft. Not for serious students.

Franklin Pierce College is a new college, very small, about 1,000 students. They offer some ceramics courses and metalcraft. This is, however, not a serious crafts place.

Strawberry Banke is a non-profit educational institution dedicated to preserving the traditions of the past. In the 1790s Simeon Lowell of Amesbury, Massachusetts, founded his boat works and, according to local and regional tradition, the family firm is credited with creating the famous Banke dory later in that decade. Today at Strawberry Banke, Ralph Lowell—the seventh generation member of his family to build small wooden craft by hand—continues to demonstrate this nearly lost art, using the tools and techniques of his ancestors. These master boat builders are assisted by apprentices to ensure the survival of this craft. There is one apprentice at the moment, but they are hoping for more.

Addresses

Arts and Science Center
41 East Pearly Street
Nashua, New Hampshire
03060
603-883-1506

Director of Admisssions
Colby College
New London, New Hampshire
03257
603-526-2010

Director of Admissions
Franklin Pierce College
Rindge, New Hampshire
03461
603-899-5111

Manchester Institute of Arts
148 Concord Street
Manchester, New Hampshire
03104
603-623-0313

Director of Admissions
Notre Dame College
2321 Elm Street
Manchester, New Hampshire
03104
603-669-4298

Sharon Arts Center
Peterborough Post Office
Sharon, New Hampshire
03458
603-924-3582

Ralph Lowell
Strawberry Banke, Inc.
P.O. Box 300
Portsmouth, New Hampshire
03842
603-436-8010

Additional Information

League of New Hampshire
Craftsmen
205 North Main Street
Concord, New Hampshire
03301
603-228-8151

Executive Director
New Hampshire Commission on
the Arts
3 Capitol Street
Concord, New Hampshire
03301
609-292-6130

NEW JERSEY

The most interesting place in New Jersey is the *Peters Valley Craft Village*. It's a small crossroad town in the mountains of northwestern New Jersey about one mile east of the Delaware River, and lies within the boundaries of the Delaware Water Gap National Recreation Park. In 1970 the National Park Service and the New Jersey State Council on the Arts formed with a group of private individuals Peters Valley Craftsmen, a non-profit, tax-exempt, educational organization. Peters Valley Craft Village is a living center devoted to education in handcrafts of all kinds. Skilled craftsmen live year-round in the village, producing, demonstrating, teaching and selling their work. Craft courses taught are ceramics, weaving, jewelry and woodcarving. Classes are kept small, no more than ten students, and are offered during a winter session and in the summer. Dormitory space is provided for about thirty people and it is possible to camp out near the village. It's a friendly and close village, a good place to work and learn.

Another interesting spot is Patricia Yuhas' *Wool Farm* near Martinsville. Patricia has a seven-acre sheep farm which she and her husband run. She writes, "It's like we were the Pilgrims who just landed. What has evolved from a back-to-the-land project is a revival of old tools and crafts with some ecological overtones. We use whatever is available and don't waste a thing." At the farm Patricia raises and shears sheep, and teaches natural dyeing to individuals and groups. She also teaches a course in dye and runs a gallery in a barn across the road from the farm. Patricia studied at the Art Student's League and the Laboratory Institute of Merchandising in New York, then she worked in textiles and weaving for Saks Fifth Avenue and McCalls before setting up the farm. It is one of the few places where students can still learn these great old skills.

Weiss Studio in Basking Ridge has been around a while—opened in 1948—and offers private and short courses in pottery, weaving, metal enameling, stitchery, stained glass and batik. All courses are taught by practicing craftsmen. Courses are eight weeks; one three-hour session per week. *Earth and Fire Ceramics Studio* in Morristown has extensive courses in ceramics, that's all.

Stitch Witchery has only stitchery and macramé, hobby approaches. The *Salem Craftsmen Guild* offers a bit more: ceramics, weaving and batik. Can do advance work here.

Other museum schools are the *Newark Museum* which has classes in ceramics, weaving and rug techniques. (Patricia Yuhas teaches here.) Standard fare, but the small faculty tries to be experimental and puts emphasis on individual creativity. Besides the classes the studios are open for use during the week, not a common practice of museum operations. *Montclair Art Museum* has ceramics and weaving, but the weaving courses are really offered at Caldwell College. Not much here.

Caldwell College has some general courses in ceramics, weaving, woodcarving, metalwork. These courses aren't for any concentration, just to prepare the students—women only—for teaching art in school. We wouldn't recommend the place. *Jersey City State College* has in their Department of Art a major for students who want to study crafts in depth. The craft possibilities are: jewelry, ceramics, weaving, textile design. This school is not known, but for New Jersey students it's a place you'd do well to check out.

Middlesex County College is a small two-year place, new, and not much for craftsmen. They have weaving and ceramics, that's all and that's not enough. *Montclair State College* has a School of Fine and Performing Arts and within this area they offer courses in ceramics, weaving, metals, and a few other crafts. The major emphasis of the department is on interart projects and interdisciplinary studies. Crafts alone is just a small part of the total curriculum. But you can earn a BA in crafts, that's an advantage.

The Fine Arts Department at *Newark State College* has a major, but the school is really only for teachers. Ceramics, jewelry, weaving and textile design are taught. Some advanced work. All that *Salem County Community College* has is glassblowing. Go there part-time for that class.

Trenton State College in rural New Jersey and on a wooded campus has a fairly complete crafts major. Courses are ceramics, jewelry, textiles and design. The place is a bit uptight and there is a long process for admissions. The Art Department for some reason wants to "observe the candidate's general appearance and poise, his manner of speech and use of language." We don't know what that has to do with arts or crafts. We'd avoid it.

Addresses

Director of Admissions
Caldwell College
Caldwell, New Jersey
07006
201-228-4424

Earth and Fire Ceramics Studio
20 Morris Street
Morristown, New Jersey
07960
201-539-9868

Director of Admissions
Jersey City State College
2039 Kennedy Boulevard
Jersey City, New Jersey
07305
201-547-3234

Director of Admissions
Middlesex County College
Woodbridge Avenue
Edison, New Jersey
08817
201-548-6000

Montclair Art Museum
South Mountain and Bloomfield
Avenues
Montclair, New Jersey
07042
201-746-5555

Director of Admissions
Montclair State College
Upper Montclair, New Jersey
07043
201-893-5116

Newark Museum
43 Washington Street

Newark, New Jersey
07101
201-733-6600

Director of Admissions
Newark State College
Union, New Jersey
07083
201-527-2000

Peters Valley Craftsmen
Peters Valley
Layton, New Jersey
07851
201-984-5200

Director of Admissions
Salem County Community College
P.O. Box 551
Penns Grove, New Jersey
08069
609-299-2100

Salem Craftsmen Guild
1042 Salem Road
Union, New Jersey
07083
201-688-3163

Stitch Witchery
Rt. 10
Box N,
Denville, New Jersey
07834
201-366-7013

Director of Admissions
Trenton State College
Trenton, New Jersey
08625
609-771-1855

*Weiss Studio and Crafts
Workshop
161 Culberson Road
Basking Ridge, New Jersey
07920
201-766-1323*

*Patricia Yuhas
Wool Farm
1020 Washington Valley Road
Martinsville, New Jersey
08836
201-356-8471*

Additional Information

*Executive Director
New Jersey State Council on the
Arts
27 West State Street
Trenton, New Jersey
08608
609-292-6130*

NEW MEXICO

The *Espiritu Libre-Cross Cultural Center for Crafts and Natural Science* emphasizes a program of training in the basic craft media and related natural sciences. It's possible to learn about textiles, clay, metal and wood. But only for beginners. *Folk Arts Workshop* has instruction in enameling. Not much more. *Turley Forge* is one of the few places in the United States where one can learn blacksmithing. Students learn the smithing essentials of drawing, upsetting, hot rasping, forge welding, punching, bending and tempering. Attempts are made to tailor the work to the individual's interests: ornamental iron (traditional or contemporary), sculptural effects, toolsmithing and jewelry. Horseshoeing work is limited to those who wish to study forging techniques. The instruction is limited to five students at a time and the shop is equipped and set up circa 1915.

New Mexico Highlands University has both a BA and an MA. This is one of the few colleges that gives crafts an equal billing with fine arts. Metals, jewelry, ceramics and weaving are taught. A small faculty but very cooperative. *New Mexico State University* in Las Cruces has a bigger program with a BA, BFA and MA, but is not that committed to crafts. Metals, jewelry and ceramics are taught. The *University of New Mexico* at Albuquerque is a large college. They offer the BFA, MA and MFA. The program here is larger, the faculty big and all the equipment you want. Plastics, enameling, metal, silversmithing, jewelry and ceramics are all taught. This is just a big state school. New Mexico is also a location that attracts a large number of independent craftsmen.

Addresses

Espiritu Libre-Cross Cultural
Center for Crafts and Natural
Sciences
P.O. Box 1841
Santa Fe, New Mexico
87501
505-455-7612

Director
Folk Arts Workshop
Route 4
Box 58 Z
Santa Fe, New Mexico
87501

Director of Admissions
New Mexico Highlands University
Las Vegas, New Mexico
87701
505-425-7511

Director of Admissions
New Mexico State University
Las Cruces, New Mexico
88001
505-646-0111

Turley Forge
P.O. Box 2051
Santa Fe, New Mexico
87501
505-983-6986

Director of Admissions
University of New Mexico
Albuquerque, New Mexico
87106
505-277-2446

Individual Instruction

BATIK

Peter Walker
801 Palisades Drive N.W.
Albuquerque, New Mexico
87105
505-242-1759

BATIK, STITCHERY

Theodora A. Tomson
Box 507
Mesilla Park, New Mexico
88047
505-526-6840

Joe Behoski
Kit Carson Museum
Cimarron, New Mexico
87714

CERAMICS

Milt Alter
12105 Bermuda N.E.
Albuquerque, New Mexico
87108
505-296-3031

Carl E. Paak
1719 Notre Dame N.E.
Albuquerque, New Mexico
87106
505-255-8162

Ralph Pardington
1503 Llano Street
Santa Fe, New Mexico
87501
505-982-9303

ENAMELS

Betty John
Box 313
Regina, New Mexico
87046
505-289-3317

FABRICS

Melanie Alter
12105 Bermuda N.E.
Albuquerque, New Mexico
87108
505-296-3031

Barbara Armstrong
1909 Morris Street N.E.
Albuquerque, New Mexico
87112
505-295-0174

Thom Barker
113 Romero N.W.
Albuquerque, New Mexico
87104
505-242-6802

Mary Bisbee
700 Camino Militar
Santa Fe, New Mexico
87501
505-983-1151

Judith Weichsel Carr
1224 Columbia N.E.
Albuquerque, New Mexico
87106
505-268-6821

Dee Henion
425 Aliso Drive N.E.
Albuquerque, New Mexico
87108
505-265-4396

Mary Elizabeth McDonald
No. 14, Nob Hill Center
3500 Central S.E.
Albuquerque, New Mexico
87108
505-266-0777

GLASSBLOWING

Ken Johnston
404 San Felipe N.W.
Albuquerque, New Mexico
87104
505-842-0403

JEWELRY

Theresa Archibeque
P.O. Box 7334
Albuquerque, New Mexico
87104
505-842-0452

Antonio Armijo
224 Bryn Mawr S.E.
Albuquerque, New Mexico
87106
505-268-6100

Robert Ayre
Hiway 10/14 North and 44
Sandia Park, New Mexico
87047
505-282-5217

Worth Long
9830 McKnight N.E.
Albuquerque, New Mexico
87112
505-299-0425

Charlie Rogers
Box 183
Mesilla Park, New Mexico
88047
505-523-0535

Individual Instruction (Cont.)

Tom W. Tomason
400 San Felipe N.W.
Albuquerque, New Mexico
87104
505-247-8311

METALWORK

Alleene Moore Chandler
1237 San Jose Avenue
Santa Fe, New Mexico
87501
505-983-8582

Bill Howell
Box 514
Ribera, New Mexico
87560

NEEDLEWORK

Eula Madsen
220 McKenzie Street
Santa Fe, New Mexico
87501
505-982-4042

NEEDLEWORK AND
LEATHER

Mary Lou Cook
Shidoni in Tesuque
New Mexico
87574
505-983-2894

POTTERY

Ann Krestensen
P.B. 586
Placitas, New Mexico
87043
505-867-2812

Helen Rumpel
320 Cadiz Road
Santa Fe, New Mexico
87501
505-982-2876

POTTERY (STONEWARE)

Bill and Kate Scranton
Box 252
Edgewood, New Mexico
87015
505-282-3774

Jean Bolton
Box 3
Miami, New Mexico
87729
505-483-5581

Jim Hunt
Hiway 44
Sandia Park, New Mexico
87047
505-282-5181

POTTERY AND
WEAVING

Santa Maria el Mirador
Box 81
Alcalde, New Mexico
87511
505-852-4244

QUILLING

Bernice T. Umland
Shidoni in Tesuque
New Mexico
87574
505-988-1737

SILVERSMITH

LoRheda Fry
Box 741
Santa Fe, New Mexico
87501
505-983-8700

Bobbie Miller
613 C Canyon Road
Santa Fe, New Mexico
87501
505-982-9131

Charles L. Myers
417 Lafayette Place N.E.
Albuquerque, New Mexico
87106
505-265-7293

Jo Roper
P.O. Box 6
Montezuma, New Mexico
87731
505-425-6033

STAINED GLASS

Ruth Almy
115 Camino Santiago
Santa Fe, New Mexico
87501
505-983-1924

James L. Hollis
Box 36
Miami, New Mexico
87729
505-483-5581

Arthur J. Tatkoski
4801 Northride Court N.E.
Albuquerque, New Mexico
87109
505-299-8113

STITCHERY

Jo Diggs
Box 578
Corrales, New Mexico
87048
505-898-5772

Wilcke Smith
3613 Dakota N.E.
Albuquerque, New Mexico
87110
505-299-9383

Cynthia A. Streck
909 Fourth
Las Vegas, New Mexico
87701
505-425-3962

WEAVING

Winifred Bream
115 Circle Drive
Santa Fe, New Mexico
87501
505-983-1534

WEAVING (CUSTOM)

Sandi Schmidt
Plaza San Ysidro
Corrales, New Mexico
87047
505-898-9947

Lucy Ann Warner
1908 Griegos Road N.W.
Albuquerque, New Mexico
87107
505-345-1480

WEAVING (HAND)

Reita R. Jordan
6901 Guadalupe Tr. N.W.
Albuquerque, New Mexico
87107
505-344-5773

Betty Meador
9600 Euclid N.E.
Albuquerque, New Mexico
87112
505-299-1472

Jan Parker
6901 Guadalupe Trail N.W.
Albuquerque, New Mexico
87107
505-344-5773

WEAVING (PUEBLO)

Lucy Yepa Lowden
2205 Wilma Road N.W.
Albuquerque, New Mexico
87104
505-247-9237

Individual Instruction (Cont.)

WELDING

Louis Baudoin
9416 Parsifal Place N.E.
Albuquerque, New Mexico
87111
505-296-5741

WOODWORK

Federico Armijo
716 Commercial S.E.
Albuquerque, New Mexico
87102
505-243-5887

Robert Burdsal
844 43rd Street
Los Alamos, New Mexico
87544
505-662-3878

Max F. Chavez
301 Arno S.E.
Albuquerque, New Mexico
87102
505-242-2935

Ralph Mondragon
Ranchos de Taos
Taos, New Mexico
87557
505-758-3644

Juan A. Romero
P.O. Box 25
Vadito, New Mexico
87579
505-587-2505

Skip Stepleton
110 Rancho Seco Road N.W.
Albuquerque, New Mexico
87104
505-242-1650

Seymour Tubis
414 Canyon Road
Santa Fe, New Mexico
87501
505-983-9607

Additional Information

Executive Director
New Mexico Arts Commission
Lew Wallace Building
Santa Fe, New Mexico
87501
505-827-2061

New Mexico Arts and Crafts Fair
Box 8801

Albuquerque, New Mexico
87108

New Mexico Designer Craftsmen
10425 Hendrix North East
Albuquerque, New Mexico
87111

NEW YORK

The *Adult Program* of the *Great Neck Public Schools* has within a section of the curriculum some craft courses. Classes are in enameling, jewelry, ceramics, wood, weaving, spinning, etc. All beginning stuff. *Charlotte Malten Ceramics Studio* has classes in ceramics, all aspects. *Clay Art Center* in Port Chester also has courses in ceramics.

College of New Rochelle has classes in jewelry, ceramics and weaving. This is a fine arts college. *Corning Community College* has some general crafts, mostly ceramics. And they do offer classes in glass engraving. *Craftsmen Unlimited* is mainly a weaving workshop, all levels and all areas. Plus they teach quilting, bobbin lace, découpage and more.

Dutchess Community College in Poughkeepsie has plastics, metal, mosaics and crafts in general. Nothing much. *Garrison Art Center* has craft courses in pottery, weaving, jewelry and metalwork. The center is non-profit and hobby levels.

Hofstra University has only a few craft classes: ceramics, metalsmithing. This is a fine arts place. Metalsmithing is the best craft here. *Kirkland College* in Clinton is a new women's college. They have some crafts: glassblowing, metal, ceramics and wood. The crafts program here is limited, but this is a new and exciting college. *Lighthouse School of Art* operates, they write, "on the concept that only through the student's own creative effect, creative growth for the individual is encouraged." Students then work a great deal on their own and instruction is limited to basic techniques and to answer individual problems. This is a fine arts place, but jewelry, pottery and weaving are taught.

Manhattanville College in Purchase, New York, is a Catholic college that has lately been going under all sorts of curriculum changes. Crafts, however, are still not that important to the school. You can take courses in textiles, weaving, batik and tie-dye. All limited in scope.

Marymount College is another women's college, Catholic in background. They offer a BA in ceramics, called a studio art major. Some other crafts: weaving, wood, stitchery. Not all that exciting. *Munson-Williams-Proctor Institute School of Art* is in Utica—a place to begin work in crafts. They teach ceramics and metal, and that's all. It's a private, non-profit place.

The *School for American Craftsmen* of the Rochester Institute of Technology offers a concentration in ceramics, metalcrafts and jewelry, weaving and textile design, and woodworking and furniture design. After two years an Associate in Applied Science Degree is granted. If students have the aptitude and interest they can study for the four-year BFA. The objectives of the School for American Craftsmen are "to provide for creative growth, the development of professional competence, and intellectual and cultural enrichment." This is one of the very best places to study crafts in the United States. It's as simple as that. Difficult to get into and you've got to be serious about your craft and your life. If you can make it, go here.

Rockland Foundation Community Art Center is a non-profit place that teaches some crafts at the hobby level. You can study glass, enameling, jewelry, ceramics and stitchery. Really not very much. *Rosary Hill College* has a BFA in ceramics and a BS in ceramics, metal and creative textiles. Courses are geared toward teaching in elementary and secondary schools.

Skidmore College in Saratoga Springs is mainly a fine arts school but they have courses in ceramics, enameling, jewelry. This is a very old art school and a very good one; crafts take second place. *St. Lawrence University* in Canton has one or two ceramics courses. Nothing. *St. Thomas Aquinas College* has jewelry, ceramics and textiles. The ceramics is the only worthwhile course here.

State University College at Buffalo has a BS degree in design. Students can major in ceramics, jewelry, metalsmithing, textiles and wood. Students concentrate in two areas in the upper division years. This is a good program, but not the best in the state. *State University College at Brockport* also has BS and BA degrees in metal, silversmithing, jewelry, ceramics and furniture. It's a program similar to Buffalo's. *State University College at Cortland* has enameling, jewelry, ceramics, and textile design, but only as a major. *State University College at Geneseo* has only a few craft courses: jewelry, ceramics, textile, wood. *State University College at New Paltz* has a BFA in silversmithing, jewelry and ceramics. This program prepares teachers for the most part. *State University of New York at Albany* offers some courses: plastics, enameling, metal, silversmithing, jewelry and ceramics. Not that much for a college this big.

State University of New York, Division of Art and Design at

Alfred University is both a private and public institution. It's the place to go for ceramics. Its College of Ceramics is a statutory unit of the SUNY system. It is difficult to think of a better place to study ceramics: here the whole college is devoted to the research, development and practice of throwing pots. It offers degrees in ceramic engineering, ceramic science, and ceramic art. At the undergraduate level the college has about 600 students. There's also a graduate program, including a PhD. The BFA program has a two-year foundation program which deals with art history and the liberal arts, some studio work. The upper levels are more flexible. This school is hard to get into; apply early.

The *College of Visual and Performing Arts* of Syracuse University is another fine place in upstate New York. They have a BFA in metal, ceramics, textile design and weaving. This college has all the facilities and equipment needed, plus a happy atmosphere. Look into Syracuse.

The *Art Center* of Albany has some hobby courses in stitchery, off-loom weaving and loom weaving. Nothing very much here.

The *Naples Hill School of Arts and Crafts* is something else indeed! It was founded as a non-profit corporation in April, 1972, and is located in the Bristol Hills in the heart of western New York's Finger Lakes region. The town of Naples is a quiet place best known for its vineyards. The Naples Hill School focuses on the individual's desires and does not pattern itself after a normal school in either curriculum demands or yearly schedules. For example, the study of only one medium is allowed during each session and studios remain open twenty-four hours a day. Major concentrations are glassblowing, ceramics, blacksmithing, textiles and batiking. There are four summer sessions and during the fall and spring extended twelve-week concentrations. This is a new and very fine attempt to establish a community of artists. A place to go, at least for the summer.

Westchester Art Workshop is part of the county of Westchester's Department of Parks. This is an adequate workshop with skilled teachers. Some serious work can be done, though lots of "leisure time" folks here. Everything is part-time, mostly more classes. The crafts offered are ceramics, jewelry, silversmithing, enameling and weaving.

The New York State Craftsmen has a new Apprentice-Training Program that offers working craftsmen and potential apprentices in New York State a central agency for referral and counseling. It's a service needed by serious craftsmen. Contact them for application forms.

Addresses

The Art Center
1069 New Scotland Road
Albany, New York
12208
518-438-8428

Clay Art Center
40 Beech Street
Port Chester, New York
10573
914-939-9508

Charlotte Malten
Ceramics Studio
193 Germonds Road
West Nyack, New York
10994
914-623-3235

Director of Admissions
College of New Rochelle
New Rochelle, New York
10801
914-632-5300

Director of Admissions
College of Visual and Performing Arts
Syracuse University
Syracuse, New York
13210
315-476-5541

Director of Admissions
Corning Community College
Corning, New York
14830
607-962-9011

Craftsmen Unlimited
16 Main Street
Bedford Hills, New York
10507
914-666-9250

Director of Admissions
Dutchess Community College
Pendell Road
Poughkeepsie, New York
12601
914-471-4500

Garrison Art Center
Box 4
Garrison, New York
10524
914-737-2168

Adult Program
Great Neck Public Schools
10 Arrandale Avenue
Great Neck, New York
11024
516-482-8659

Director of Admissions
Hofstra University
Hempstead, New York
11550
516-560-0500

Director of Admissions
Kirkland College
Clinton, New York
13323
315-859-7462

Lighthouse School of Art
659 Route 9W
Upper Grandview, New York
10960
914-359-2151

Director of Admissions
Manhattanville College
Purchase, New York
10577
914-946-9600

Director of Admissions
Marymount College
Tarrytown, New York
10591
914-631-3451

Munson-Williams-Proctor
Institute
310 Genesee Street
Utica, New York
13502
315-797-0000

The Naples Mills School
33 Academy Street
Post Box 567
Naples, New York
14512
315-374-2478

Rockland Center for the Arts
27-29 Old Greenbush Road
West Nyack, New York
10994
914-358-0877

Director of Admissions
Rosary Hill College
4380 Main Street
Buffalo, New York
14226
716-839-3600

Director of Admissions
St. Lawrence University
Canton, New York
13617
315-379-5011

Director of Admissions
St. Thomas Aquinas College
Sparkill, New York
10976
914-359-1279

Director of Admissions
School of the American Craftsmen
Rochester Institute of Technology
One Lomb Memorial Drive
Rochester, New York
14623
716-464-2831

Director of Admissions
Skidmore College
Saratoga Springs, New York
12866
518-584-5000

Director of Admissions
SUNY—Albany
1400 Washington Avenue
Albany, New York
12222
518-457-8996

Director of Admissions
SUNY—Alfred University
Alfred, New York
14802
607-871-2115

Director of Admissions
SUNY—Brockport
Brockport, New York
14420
716-395-2211

Director of Admissions
SUNY—Buffalo
1300 Elmwood Avenue
Buffalo, New York
14222
716-862-4000

Director of Admissions
SUNY—Cortland
Cortland, New York
13045
607-753-2011

Addresses (Cont.)

Director of Admissions
SUNY—Geneseo
Geneseo, New York
14454
716-245-5211

Director of Admissions
SUNY—New Paltz
New Paltz, New York
12561
914-257-2121

Registrar
Westchester Art Workshop
County Center
White Plains, New York
10606
212-949-1300

Individual Instruction

WEAVING

Raymonde Bostwick
Rt 1 Box 46
Annandale Road
Red Hook, New York
12571
914-758-8617

Helen Brown
1321 Pinnacle Road
Henrietta, New York
14467

Ruth Castino
34 Hamilton Avenue
Sloatsburg, New York
10974
914-753-5105

Additional Information

Executive Director
New York State Council on the
Arts
250 West 57th Street
New York, New York
10019
212-586-2040

Harry Dennis, Jr.,
Executive Director
New York State Craftsmen
P.O. Box 733
Ithaca, New York
14850

NEW YORK CITY

Adventures in Crafts has some hobby-type classes in découpage, repoussé and glass. *Paula Adler* in the lower West Village has classes in weaving and related fiber techniques. Classes meet once a week. Paula is a well-known New York weaver. *Art Life Craft Studios* teaches ceramics and wood; it's a small, private place mainly given over to artistic aims. Okay, but you can do better in the city. The *Art Students League* on the West Side has courses in textile design. This is a very good place for textiles. The *Arts and Crafts Program of the Riverside Church* is an extensive program, but limited in terms of advancement. It's possible to study batik and tie-dyeing, bookbinding, ceramics, enameling, jewelry, quilting, glass, weaving, yarn spinning and natural dyeing. First-class instructors.

Baldwin Pottery is a workshop for professional and semi-professional potters and also a school for adults and children. They offer intensive courses in throwing, handbuilding and glazing. Very good facilities and teachers. The *Bronx Community College* offers an AA degree in crafts, mainly to prepare you to do further study. Courses are limited in crafts. Really not that valuable. *Brooklyn Museum Art School* writes, "At our school nothing gets between you and your art. There are no formal requirements. If you have the desire and talent, we're interested. There are no grades. There are no large classes. In other words, the atmosphere is that of a community of working artists." You can study all crafts here. Good place.

The *Craft Institute of America* on East 75th has an extensive and excellent program in all crafts. Everything is available here! Instruction is excellent and the place is friendly. *Craft Students League of the West Side YWCA* has an international reputation as a center for avocational and vocational training in crafts. It has the largest selection of classes in the city. All the instruction is first-rate. A place to attend.

Designs in Clay has courses in ceramics, nothing much. *Allen and Dorothy Fannin* are full-time craftsmen who do take apprentices. They are outstanding craftsmen who consult with several craft programs in the East. It is possible that you might be able to work out an apprentice program with them.

Fashion Institute of Technology is an outstanding school, fully accredited, that has a textile design course leading to an AA degree. The program includes the designing of printed, woven and knitted fabrics and other materials. A highly professional program and well worth it. *Grand Street Potters* offers all classes in pottery, beginning through Japanese ceramics. Courses are inexpensive but they have tight rules and regulations. (For example, you can't make up classes if you miss.) *Greenwich House Pottery* is an old and established school specializing in pottery and sculpture classes for children and adults. Classes are kept small and students progress individually. Very fine faculty, good place to learn. *Henry Street Settlement School of Art and Pottery* is a craft opportunity for people on the Lower East Side. Mostly for beginning students. Courses are ceramics, batik and tie dye. Instruction is more than adequate.

Hunter College has a few courses: metal, ceramics, plastics, textile design, wood. This is a fine arts college, not really for the craftsman. *Mrs. Laura Young* is a hand bookbinder and one of the very best in America. She has been teaching for over twenty-five years and takes private students who, she writes, "receive personal and individual instruction in the areas of their interests." This is one of the few places in the country where you can study bookbinding in a concentrated way.

Mavros Workshop offers classes in wheel pottery, hand building, ceramic sculpture and glaze chemistry. It is run by Donald Odysseus Mavros, who is a well-known sculptor, ceramist, painter and teacher. First-class place. The *New School for Social Research* has craft courses in just about everything. This is a very good school, in all aspects, has an excellent faculty, and is expensive! Can study knitting, American Indian beadwork, quillwork and appliqué, plus ceramics, jewelry, weaving, etc. There are also courses like, How to Sell Your Crafts. Can't go wrong here. *New York University* has a few classes in crafts: plastics, jewelry, wood, weaving, stitchery. Not really worthwhile.

The *Pot Shop* is run by Doris Licht-Tomono. She teaches general ceramics and glaze calculation in her own studio. Classes are limited to ten students and the courses are inexpensive. Excellent facilities. *Pratt Institute of Technology* is another excellent New York City school. A BFA and MFA in ceramics are offered, plus courses in metal, textiles and textile design. Can't go wrong here.

Rose H. Sulymoss Studio is one of the few studios where one can learn the art of monumental sculpture. Instruction is on apprentice-type basis. The *School of Batik Painting* is another unusual place. It is an experimental institution for the cultivation of batik as a medium of fine art, associated with the movement of the New School of Batik in India. All students are trained according to their individual abilities. The courses are all short and students earn a certificate if they can pass the examinations.

School of Visual Arts is an energetic place mainly concerned with fine art areas. They do, however, have courses in textile design. This is a good place to study, fully accredited. *Spencer Depas Studio* has weaving classes for beginners and advanced students. Beginners are taught how to set up the loom and various weaving techniques. Advanced students learn wall hangings of various types, or tapestry weaving. Rug-making can also be taken. Some macramé is taught, but by arrangement. *Studio Del, School of Crochet Art* is conducted by Del Pitt Feldman who recently published *Crochet: Discovery and Design*. The three areas of crochet are: creating clothing, three-dimensional sculpture and ornamental wall hangings.

Teachers College of Columbia University has courses in enameling, metal, jewelry, ceramics and textile design. All limited and just to prepare high school teachers. *Wagner College* on Staten Island has a few courses in ceramics. And at the *92nd Street YM–YWHA* courses are given in glass, metal, ceramics and textile designs. Elementary levels.

Addresses

Paula Adler
228 West Houston Street
New York, New York
10014
212-989-7327

Adventures in Crafts
218 East 81st Street
New York, New York
10028
212-628-8081

Art Life Craft Studios
1384 Third Avenue
New York, New York
10021
212-535-0840

Art Students League
215 West 57th Street
New York, New York
10021
212-247-4510

Addresses (Cont.)

Arts and Crafts Program
Riverside Church
490 Riverside Drive
New York, New York
10027
212-749-8140

Baldwin Pottery
540 Laguardia Place
New York, New York
10012
212-475-7236

Director of Admissions
Bronx Community College
120 East 184th Street
Bronx, New York
10468
212-960-8616

Brooklyn Museum Art School
200 Eastern Parkway
Brooklyn, New York
11238
212-638-4486

Craft Institute of America
330 East 75th Street
New York, New York
10021

Craft Students League
YWCA
840 Eighth Avenue
New York, New York
10019
212-246-4712

Designs in Clay
327 West 11th Street
New York, New York
10014

Allen and Dorothy Fannin
P.O. Box 376 GPO
Brooklyn, New York
11201
212-768-6079

Director of Admissions
Fashion Institute of Technology
227 West 27th Street
New York, New York
10001
212-594-0390

Grand Street Potters
135 Grand Street
New York, New York
10013
212-431-9271

Greenwich House Pottery
16 Jones Street
New York, New York
10014
212-242-4106

Henry Street Settlement School
265 Henry Street
New York, New York
10002
212-962-1100

Director of Admissions
Hunter College
695 Park Avenue
New York, New York
10021
212-360-5566

Mavros Workshop
49 West 28th Street
New York, New York
10001
212-689-1097

Director of Admissions
New School for Social Research
66 West 12th Street
New York, New York
10011
212-675-2700

Director of Admissions
New York University
80 Washington Square

New York, New York
10003
212-598-3127

Pot Shop
Doris Licht-Tomono
356 Bowery
New York, New York
10012
212-473-0182

Director of Admissions
Pratt Institute of Technology
200 Grand Avenue
Brooklyn, New York
11205
212-622-2200

School of Batik Painting
64 West 84th Street
New York, New York
10024
212-595-1126

Director of Admissions
School of Visual Arts
209 East 23rd Street
New York, New York
10010
212-679-7350

Spencer Dépas Studio
227 Cumberland Street
Brooklyn, New York
11205
212-852-8122

Studio Del
School of Crochet

19 East 7th Street
New York, New York
10003
212-228-7130

Rose H. Sulymoss Studio
32 Union Square
New York, New York
10003
212-473-1382

Director of Admissions
Teachers College
Columbia University
New York, New York
10027
212-870-4200

Director of Admissions
Wagner College
Howard Avenue
Staten Island, New York
10301
212-390-3000

Education Department
YM & YWHA
1395 Lexington Avenue
New York, New York
10028
212-427-6000

Mrs. Laura S. Young
601 West 115th Street
New York, New York
10025
212-864-0141

NORTH CAROLINA

In this state the place to go is, of course, *Penland*. Here's one of those Mecca places for crafts people, especially in the summer. It is very very hard to get into, not because of skill but because so many people apply. One really shouldn't apply here unless they've been in crafts awhile; you're wasting everyone's time, but Penland does accept, as they say, "rank beginners."

The school grew out of a community handcraft endeavor started in 1923 by Lucy Morgan. At the time Edward Worst of Chicago was the foremost authority on handweaving and he came one summer to give a course to the community weavers. Then others heard about the school and started to write. The school actually started in 1929 with seven students. It gets bigger every year. Just about everyone who is famous in crafts has taught at Penland. To name a few: Toshiko Takaezu, Robert Turner (ceramics); Janet Taylor and Jean Stamsta (weaving); Thomas Gentille (metal-jewelry); Hede von Nagel (enameling); Sam Maloof (woodwork); Joel Myers (glassblowing).

Penland recently opened a new concentrated program. It consists of two eight-week sessions, fall and spring. All classes are limited. In ceramics, textiles, glassblowing, and jewelry-metal-smithing. It's expensive—over $360.00 for tuition; room and board runs about $560.00 for the eight weeks. But it's worth it!

All the students are expected to "participate in the rotating shop monitoring, kiln stacking, firing and dining room duties." You have to be at least eighteen and need to submit a résumé of education and background. Apply early. The Concentration Session is limited to fifty-eight students.

There's a good book on Penland titled *Gift from the Hills,* the whole story of the school. It's available in paperback from Penland.

Also in North Carolina is the very important and unique *John C. Campbell Folk School.* It is to my knowledge the only operating Grundtvigian folk school in the United States. It was founded in 1925 "to pioneer the adaptation of folk school educational principles to conditions in the Southern Highland region of the U.S." Out of this has come a demonstration farm, a woodcarving enterprise, short courses in crafts and recreation and service-learning programs for youth. The Folk School is for young people, 18 to 30 years of age.

The heart of the Folk School is the winter term, January through May. It is all group living and learning-by-doing. Many of the students come from other colleges and make arrangements for credit, etc., but quite a few others just come on their own. There are four major areas of activities: community development (service-learning internships) ; recreation (folk dancing, singing, folklore, music) ; farming (dairy, greenhouse, etc.) ; and crafts (woodcarving, woodworking, weaving, lapidary) .

There are a series of short courses scattered throughout the remainder of the year. It is possible for younger students—minimum age of 16—to take two-week craft courses. Students are accepted from all over, but they try to encourage local participation.

What makes the Folk School's craft classes and courses special is that an active, respected, permanent craft cottage industry is fostered by the school and that the crafts, for the most part, are native to the area. Several of the teachers are traditional or locally trained craftsmen.

Writing to us about the school, the director, John Ramsay, said, "We live in buildings made of native wood and stone. We soak up the beauty of fields and forests and mountain ranges, including the Smokies and Blue Ridge Mountains, as we go about our work. Staff and non-staff eat together for the noon meals during the week. Our home-grown meals have been part of the Folk School reputation for years. Students stay in houses having rooms with one to three beds each. Working together makes a 'join-in' atmosphere. Participants take part in both daily chores and occasional group work projects such as hauling hay, stacking lumber at the sawmill, doing maintenance or cleaning, or preparing meals." All that and you learn a craft!

Not far from the J. C. Campbell Folk School in Brasstown is the *Kelischek Workshop* for historical instruments. Here's a place where you can go and build yourself a musical instrument such as a viola da gamba, rebec, lute, hurdy-gurdy, psaltery, dulcimer, violin, guitar, vielle, kelhorn, krummhorn or harpsichord.

You can register at any time of the year and stay as long as you want (or need) to finish your instrument. All of this costs about $35 a week. You can bring your own material or purchase kits or raw materials from the Workshop. All the tools, jigs, templates, molds, etc., are provided by the Workshop. Craftsmen with little experience in woodworking are advised to start out with a simple instrument or to use one of the advanced kits rather than raw material.

Kelischek Workshop also arranges individual lessons on the recorder, krummhorn, kelhorn, viols or keyboard instruments.

There's lodging at Fiddlers-Hall closeby the Workshop, or at the J. C. Campbell Folk School. About $3.50 a night. About themselves, they write, "Just a small community of Cherokee County, Brasstown is a place where potters, weavers, blacksmiths, wood carvers and instrument makers pursue their ancient crafts with dedication and success. A good place not only to live in, but just as good to visit and experience."

Arts and Crafts Association in Winston-Salem has introductory courses, all beginning. They tend to concentrate on hobby-type crafts, crocheting, non-loom weaving, macramé, that sort of thing. The colleges and universities have majors in crafts and they are mostly strong programs.

At *Mars Hill College* students can concentrate on studio work, but students have to spend the first two years completing introductory courses. The studio work is limited to ceramics, however. That's a major drawback of the school, but the campus is located in one of the more beautiful places in the state.

It's possible to study ceramics and metals at the *University of North Carolina at Asheville,* but there's a lot of requirements and prerequisites, including a language requirement. Not a difficult college to get into. The *University of North Carolina at Chapel Hill* has a Department of Art but it cautions, "Employment opportunities in art are extremely limited, and unless one is highly motivated, this department does not recommend matriculation in the art field." Having said this, the college offers only ceramics. The University at Chapel Hill has masters and PhD programs in art, many courses in crafts through the Penland School.

East Carolina University has BFA in ceramics, a high concentration of at least forty-five quarter-hours in the major. In fact, most of this curriculum is devoted to learning the skill. Minors can be picked up in textiles, jewelry and printmaking. This is a good place to earn a degree in crafts in North Carolina.

Gaston College is a two-year school. They have courses in jewelry and ceramics, also art appreciation. Only beginners stuff. *Elizabeth City State University* has an art major, but crafts here are limited. *Western Carolina University* in Cullowhee has a good and a wide range of craft offerings. Jewelry, woodcarving, stitchery, textiles and ceramics are all taught. *Duke University* has just ceramics, crafts not taken seriously here. *Jugtown Pottery* takes three people for four-month apprentice sessions. This is a famous design workshop in the state and hard to get into.

Addresses

Arts and Crafts Association
610 Coliseum Drive
Winston-Salem, North Carolina
27106
704-723-7395

Kelischek Workshop
Brasstown, North Carolina
28902
704-837-5833

John C. Campbell Folk School
Brasstown, North Carolina
28902
704-837-2775

Director of Admissions
Duke University
Durham, North Carolina
27708
919-684-8111

Director of Admissions
East Carolina University
Greenville, North Carolina
27834
919-758-6131

Director of Admissions
Elizabeth City State University
Elizabeth City, North Carolina
27909
919-335-0551

Director of Admissions
Gaston College
Dallas, North Carolina
28034
704-922-3136

Jugtown Pottery
Route Two
Seagrove, North Carolina
27341
919-464-3266

Director of Admissions
Mars Hill College
Mars Hill, North Carolina
28754
704-689-1151

Penland School of Crafts
Penland, North Carolina
28765
704-765-2359

Director of Admissions
University of North Carolina
Asheville, North Carolina
28804
704-254-7415

Director of Admissions
University of North Carolina
Chapel Hill, North Carolina
27514
919-933-2211

Director of Admissions
Western Carolina University
Cullowhee, North Carolina
28723
704-293-7211

Additional Information

Executive Director
North Carolina Arts Council
250 West 57th Street
New York, New York
10019
212-586-2040

Southern Highland Handicraft
Guild
15 Reddick Road
P.O. Box 9145
Asheville, North Carolina
28805

NORTH DAKOTA

Jamestown College is really a fine arts place. They have in their Art Department two courses in crafts, one general, one in beginning ceramics. Not much else. Avoid. *Minot State College* in the Division of Fine and Applied Arts has several craft courses, ceramics mainly. You can get a major here.

Addresses

Director of Admissions
Jamestown College
Jamestown, North Dakota
58401
701-252-4331

Director of Admissions
Minot State College
9th Avenue N.W.
Minot, North Dakota
58701
701-838-6101

Additional Information

North Dakota Council on the Arts
John Hove, Chairman
c/o Department of English
North Dakota State University
Fargo, North Dakota
58102
701-237-7143

OHIO

One of the best places to attend college in this state (or in the United States) is *Antioch College*. Antioch was the first (1921) liberal arts college to experiment with the educational concept of work and study. Art students at Antioch—following the theory of work-study—are now learning in one-to-one relationships with artists-craftsmen, rather than formal work assignments. Antioch students are already apprenticed to a number of potters, jewelers and other craftsmen throughout the United States. Students usually stay with an artist-craftsman for three to six months, the rest of the academic year is spent on-campus in Yellow Springs. A BA degree from Antioch takes five years. It's worth the time.

Capital University is a small Lutheran school that has some craft possibilities in their Art Department. All elementary stuff. Nothing important here. The *College of Mount St. Joseph on the Ohio* is a very Catholic, very women's college. Their Art Department is limited and traditional. Lots of ceramics are offered, some weaving, one course in metal. They train art teachers.

The *Cleveland Institute of Art* is a highly regarded school, fully accredited and granting a BFA degree in ceramics, jewelry, enameling and silversmithing, weaving and textile design. Degree program takes five years with the first two years spent in a common basic program. Difficult and first-rate place, one of the few of its kind.

The *Mansfield Art Center* throws in a few craft courses: ceramics, weaving, stitchery. Nothing important, hobby stuff. The *Toledo Museum of Art* offers some very good design classes and also a class in beginning work in glass. Other classes are in metal, ceramics. *Riverbend Art Center* has just a potpourri of craft classes, most at the beginner's level, everything from batik to woodcarving.

The *School of the Dayton Art Institute* offers a BFA, has about 200 students, all non-residents. Students must have an interview. The school is looking for highly motivated students, "who have the responsibility necessary to cope with freedom and flexibility." Craft programs in ceramics only, however. Otherwise, valuable school.

Baycrafters' classes, they write, "are designed for those who are interested in art as a recreational activity or for specialized training in some particular medium. Courses are available in just about all crafts, usually once a week and usually only for beginners.

The Working Hand Craft Center run by Philip Morton is a unique apprenticeship program. Morton produces handmade contemporary jewelry and has five apprentices. The program takes about three years and prepares students to earn a living as a hand craftsman. Philip Morton writes, "This program is no short-cut to success, but your rate of progress will depend upon your ability and your effort. You will enter at your own level." This is something for metalsmiths to consider.

Denison University is one of those very fine small colleges the Midwest is famous for. It's possible to get a BFA in ceramics here, no other crafts. The program is structured, but not too. *Edgecliff College* is a Catholic college, coeducational. They have some ceramics and weaving.

Kent State University has a Design and Crafts Division in their School of Art. BFAs and MFAs are offered. Need to be selected by school. They write, "The School of Art recognizes that unusual competence in the visual arts as well as high intellectual capacity are necessary qualities in students who plan to prepare for a career in one of the art fields." Tough to get accepted. Major crafts: glassblowing, enameling, jewelry, ceramics, weaving.

Malone College hasn't much. A few courses in ceramics. Avoid. *Miami University* has a BFA program, some crafts, but not much here. *Ohio Dominican College* is another small Catholic place. They have a couple of ceramics and textiles courses. *Ohio State University* has a BFA in ceramics. The program is "directed toward the development of individual approaches and abilities in conjunction with competent craftsmanship." Rather complete course. *Ohio University-Belmont Campus* only has ceramics and wood, general stuff. But the *School of Art, Ohio University* in Athens has it all! BFA and MFA in ceramics. Other undergraduate fields are metal, weaving and wood. Excellent place.

The College of Wooster is a Presbyterian school that offers some ceramics, in a general sort of way in the Art Department. *University of Cincinnati* has a BFA and MFA in ceramics, also enameling, jewelry. But you can do better elsewhere in the state. *Ursuline College* is yet another Catholic college and for women only. It has some ceramics, metal and enameling. Not much.

Addresses

Director of Admissions
Antioch College
Yellow Springs, Ohio
45387
513-767-7331

Baycrafters
28795 Lake Road
Huntington Reservation
Bay Village, Ohio
44140
216-871-6543

Director of Admissions
Capital University
Main Street
Columbus, Ohio
43209
614-236-6011

Director of Admissions
Cleveland Institute of Art
11141 East Boulevard
Cleveland, Ohio
44106
216-421-4322

Director of Admissions
College of Mount St. Joseph on
the Ohio
Mount St. Joseph, Ohio
45051
513-244-4200

Director of Admissions
The College of Wooster
Wooster, Ohio
44691
216-264-1234

Director of Admissions
School of the Dayton Art Institute
Forest and Riverview Avenues
Dayton, Ohio
45401
513-223-5277

Director of Admissions
Denison University
Box 149
Granville, Ohio
43023
614-582-9181

Director of Admissions
Edgecliff College
2220 Victory Parkway
Cincinnati, Ohio
45206
513-961-3770

Director of Admissions
Kent State University
150 Rockwell Hall
Kent, Ohio
44242
216-672-2444

Director of Admissions
Malone College
515 25th Street N.W.
Canton, Ohio
44709
216-454-3011

Mansfield Art Center
700 Marion Avenue
Mansfield, Ohio
44903
419-756-1700

Director of Admissions
Miami University
Oxford, Ohio
45056
513-529-2161

Director of Admissions
Ohio Dominican College
1216 Sunbury Road
Columbia, Ohio
43219
614-253-2741

Addresses (Cont.)

Director of Admissions
Ohio State University
190 North Oval Drive
Columbus, Ohio
43210
614-422-8412

Director of Admissions
Ohio University-Belmont Campus
National Road, West
St. Clairsville, Ohio
43950
614-695-1720

Director of Admissions
School of Art
Ohio University
Athens, Ohio
45701
614-594-5511

Betty L. Stringer
Riverbend Art Center
142 Riverbend Drive
Dayton, Ohio
45405
513-225-5433

School of Design
Toledo Museum of Art
P.O. Box 1013
Toledo, Ohio
43601
419-255-8000

Director of Admissions
University of Cincinnati
615 A Brodie
Cincinnati, Ohio
45221
513-475-8000

Director of Admissions
Ursuline College
2600 Lander Road
Cleveland, Ohio
44124
216-449-4200

Philip Morton
The Working Hand Craft Center
515 Conneaut
Bowling Green, Ohio
43402
419-353-9932

Additional Information

Ceramic and Craft Guild of
Greater Cincinnati
933 Avondale Avenue
Cincinnati, Ohio
45229

Executive Director
Ohio Arts Council
50 West Broad Street
Columbus, Ohio
43215
614-469-2613

OKLAHOMA

Bacone College is a junior college mainly for Indian students. The crafts program is quite good for beginning students.

Weaving, wood, silversmithing and special Indian art courses are taught. *Central State University* has just ceramics. Nothing else. *East Central State College* does better. Glassblowing is available here, plus courses in plastics, metal, jewelry, ceramics and wood. *Northeastern State College* has about the same set of classes and some furniture classes. These courses aren't organized into a degree, however.

Oklahoma State University has ceramics as an area of concentration and offers a BA and BFA. They train teachers here. Not much more is offered except some good design classes, art history and art principles. The school on the whole isn't that exciting. *Oral Roberts University* is a strongly religious place (famous for its basketball teams) that has a BA in ceramics. Nothing else. They train teachers here, too.

The other three colleges in Oklahoma that offer crafts courses aren't much better. *Phillips University* is a small religious college that has a BA in ceramics and mainly trains teachers. Their program in crafts is extensive, all major crafts are taught, but ceramics is it here. Better place to study is the *University of Oklahoma*. A BFA is given in metal, jewelry and ceramics. The main emphasis is on design. They have a large Fine Arts Department, but the curriculum is straight and not imaginative. Lastly, the *University of Tulsa* has just some "arts and crafts" courses, a few ceramics, weaving, stitchery, etc. No studio work to speak of.

As for private courses . . . there's *Contemporary Handcrafts* in Oklahoma City, which has weaving classes using frame looms, inkle looms and four-harness floor looms. Also macramé. In Norman at *Firehouse Art Station* you can take classes in ceramics, jewelry, wood and macramé. Both these places are for people new to crafts. Both are good places to begin.

Addresses

Director of Admissions
Bacone College
Bacone, Oklahoma
74420
918-683-4581

Director of Admissions
Central State University
Edmond, Oklahoma
73034
405-341-2980

Addresses (Cont.)

Contemporary Handcrafts
Paseo Design Center
2927 Paseo
Oklahoma City, Oklahoma
73103
405-525-7227

Director of Admissions
East Central State College
Ada, Oklahoma
74820
405-332-8000

Firehouse Art Station
444 South Flood
Norman, Oklahoma
73069
405-329-4523

Director of Admissions
Northeastern State College
Tahlequah, Oklahoma
74464
918-456-5511

Director of Admissions
Oklahoma State University
Stillwater, Oklahoma
74074
405-372-6211

Director of Admissions
Oral Roberts University
7777 South Lewis
Tulsa, Oklahoma
74102
918-743-6161

Director of Admissions
Phillips University
Enid, Oklahoma
73701
405-237-4433

Director of Admissions
University of Oklahoma
Norman, Oklahoma
73069
405-325-2251

Director of Admissions
University of Tulsa
600 South College
Tulsa, Oklahoma
74104
918-939-6351

Additional Information

Executive Director
Oklahoma Arts Council
Glenbrook Centre West
1140 N.W. 63rd Street
Oklahoma City, Oklahoma
73116
405-521-2660

Oklahoma Arts and Humanities
Council
Glenbrook Centre West
1140 N.W. 63rd
Oklahoma City, Oklahoma
73116
405-521-2931

OREGON

Maude Kerns is a non-profit organization serving the Eugene-Springfield community. Classes are in ceramics, all levels; textiles, jewelry and some stained glass, leather. The *School of the Arts and Crafts Society* in Portland has a very good and extensive craft program, almost everything is taught. The school is worth looking up. *Corvallis Arts Center,* formed in 1961, has a series of craft courses in pottery and weaving, taught as hobbies.

Museum Art School is the oldest full-time art school in the Pacific Northwest. It's a private school for pre-professional training, a very good school in which to begin in crafts and a place where you can earn a BFA in four years and/or take a five-year course, with one year at Reed College, to earn a teacher's certificate. This, however, is mostly a fine arts place. *Coos Art Museum* has some classes, weaving, jewelry, rug techniques, all hobby stuff.

There are some summer possibilities. One is the *Creative Arts Community,* a two-week crafts camp at Camp Menucha on the Columbia River. Classes are in metal, pottery and weaving. Another summer workshop is *Hal Painter's* camp on the Sprague River in southeastern Oregon. Workshops are in weaving and dyeing.

College programs are: *Eastern Oregon College,* which has BA and BS programs, offers a wide range of classes in their Art Department. Nothing concentrated, however. *Lewis and Clark College* has a BA in fine arts, students can major in ceramics, textiles and weaving. *Oregon College of Education* trains teachers and they have crafts, all for art teachers. Not anything here unless you want to teach. *Oregon State University* has a BA in silversmithing, ceramics and weaving. It's a big Art Department. The best equipped program at the college level in the state. *Southern Oregon College* trains teachers of art. Some crafts given.

Portland State University is the best place in Oregon to study crafts. The focus of the Department of Art is on studio work. The craft concentrations are in ceramics, weaving and metal. The college offers BAs and BSs in all crafts. There is also an MFA in ceramics. Studio space is a full block square. There are individual graduate studios. Other crafts offered are in glass and woodwork. Portland State has a large and well-qualified staff. Can't do better in Oregon than here.

Addresses

Coos Art Museum
515 Market Street
Coos Bay, Oregon
97420
503-267-3901

Corvallis Arts Center
7th and Madison
Corvallis, Oregon
97330
503-752-0186

Director of Admissions
Eastern Oregon College
La Grande, Oregon
97850
503-963-2171

Maude Kerns Art Center
1910 E. 15th Avenue
Eugene, Oregon
97403

Director of Admissions
Lewis and Clark College
615 S.W. Palatine Hill Road
Portland, Oregon
97219
503-244-6161

Museum Art School
S.W. Park and Madison Street
Portland, Oregon
97209
503-226-4391

Creative Arts Community
Oregon Council of Churches
4607 S.W. Dosch Road
Portland, Oregon
97201
503-235-5206

Hal Painter
c/o Potter's Camp
Star Route
Chiloquin, Oregon
97624

School of the Arts and Crafts
Society
616 N.W. 18th Avenue
Portland, Oregon
97209
503-228-4741

Director of Admissions
Oregon College of Education
Monmouth, Oregon
97361
503-838-1220

Director of Admissions
Oregon State University
Corvallis, Oregon
97331
503-754-0123

Director of Admissions
Portland State University
Portland, Oregon
97204
503-229-3511

Director of Admissions
Southern Oregon College
1250 Siskiyou Boulevard
Ashland, Oregon
97520
503-482-3311

Additional Information

Mr. Gordon Smyth, Director
Contemporary Crafts Association
3934 S.W. Corbett Avenue
Portland, Oregon
97201
503-223-2654

Executive Secretary
Oregon Arts Commission
328 Oregon Building
494 State Street
Salem, Oregon
97301
503-378-3625

PENNSYLVANIA

Allegheny College in Meadville is a small liberal arts place, a good school, an old-fashioned school; and they offer some ceramics in the Art Department, but not enough. *Beaver College* is a women's college and they have BFAs to offer in crafts. Mostly a fine arts place, however. Rather strict. *Bloomsburg State College* offers a BA in ceramics, weaving and textile design. This is an unnoticed state school, but its crafts program is solid, if only basic.

Carnegie-Mellon University is one of the best places to study crafts in the country. The have a BFA in metal and a BFA and MFA in ceramics and weaving. The crafts are located in the Department of Painting and Sculpture. First-class facilities, but crafts is not the center of the curriculum. You can get glassblowing, though.

Cedar Crest College is an old school, a women's college connected wth the United Church of Christ. It offers a BA in ceramics and woodcarving, also some other crafts. Small faculty and heavy concentration. Not a bad school; recently they've revised their educational program. *Chatham College* is another women's school, and a fine college, but unfortunately they have a limited program. They have ceramics, tucked away in the Art Department.

Community College of Philadelphia offers a course or two in ceramics. Not worthwhile. *Drexel University,* also in Philadelphia, has some weaving classes in their textile and merchandising course. This school has a good reputation but is not a crafts place. *East Stroudsburg State College* is another place where crafts are offered, but the offerings are limited. They have ceramics and some general stuff. That's all.

Edinboro State College is a former normal school and they're proud of it. They train teachers. The crafts program here is big, but it's all geared so the students can teach in elementary or secondary schools. Okay school if you want to teach. *Indiana University of Pennsylvania* has, as many know, one of the most beautiful campuses in America. It has a collection of craft classes, no degree. Can do better in the state, but you'll miss a nice place to go to school.

Juniata College is a small coeducational place. They have a couple of ceramics classes. Not worth it. *Kutztown State College* has a BS in art education. They offer enameling, jewelry and crafts. But it's a place for teachers. *Mansfield State College* is the best state college for crafts. Nearly every craft is taught here, but no degree in fine arts, or major. Good solid and fundamental stuff.

Moore College of Art is America's oldest college for women. It's a small school—600 students—and awards a BS in art education, a BFA and a BA in art history. You can major in ceramics, design, jewelry and metalsmithing. Very fine college, trains for a career.

Another excellent Philadelphia school is the *Philadelphia College of Art,* which has a BFA. The major studies are offered in ceramics and glass, jewelry and metalsmithing, woodworking and furniture design. "The program is geared to equip the student for professional competition." They train working craftsmen here! And again in Philadelphia is *Tyler School of Art* of Temple University. This is another outstanding school. Everything is available here: BFAs and MFAs, also blacksmithing. All students take a foundation course, second year is a general year and final two years is heavy concentration in one craft. Just a really good school.

Seton Hill College is a Catholic women's college. A BA is offered in ceramics, jewelry, weaving. Lots of independent study. *Westminster College* has ceramics, jewelry. Nothing much. And at *Wilkes College* there's metal, jewelry and ceramics.

In Pittsburgh there's the non-college craft opportunity of *Arts and Crafts Center.* Wide range of crafts, mostly beginners. Also in Pittsburgh is *The Fringe,* classes in weaving and textile techniques. Very good short courses.

Addresses

Director of Admissions
Allegheny College
Meadville, Pennsylvania
16335
814-724-3100

Director of Admissions
Arts and Crafts Center of
Pittsburgh
Fifth and Shady Avenues
Pittsburgh, Pennsylvania
15232
412-361-0873

Director of Admissions
Beaver College
Glenside, Pennsylvania
19038
215-884-3500

Director of Admissions
Bloomsburg State College
Bloomsburg, Pennsylvania
17815
717-389-0111

Director of Admissions
Carnegie-Mellon University
500 Forbes Avenue
Pittsburgh, Pennsylvania
15213
412-621-2600

Director of Admissions
Cedar Crest College
Allentown, Pennsylvania
18104
215-437-4471

Director of Admissions
Chatham College
Woodland Road
Pittsburgh, Pennsylvania
15232
412-441-8200

Director of Admissions
Community College of
Philadelphia
34 South 11th Street
Philadelphia, Pennsylvania
19107
215-569-3680

Director of Admissions
Drexel University
32nd and Chestnut Streets
Philadelphia, Pennsylvania
19104
215-387-2400

Director of Admissions
East Stroudsburg State College
East Stroudsburg, Pennsylvania
18301
717-421-4080

Director of Admissions
Edinboro State College
Edinboro, Pennsylvania
15412
814-734-1671

Director of Admissions
The Fringe
5600 Walnut Street
Pittsburgh, Pennsylvania
15232
412-441-8798

Director of Admissions
Indiana University of
Pennsylvania
Indiana, Pennsylvania
15701
412-357-2100

Director of Admissions
Juniata College
Huntingdon, Pennsylvania
16652
814-643-4310

Addresses (Cont.)

Director of Admissions
Kutztown State College
Kutztown, Pennsylvania
19530
215-683-3511

Director of Admissions
Mansfield State College
Mansfield, Pennsylvania
16933
717-662-2114

Director of Admissions
Moore College of Art
20th and Race Streets
Philadelphia, Pennsylvania
19103
215-568-4515

Director of Admissions
Philadelphia College of Art
Broad and Pine Streets
Philadelphia, Pennsylvania
19102
215-546-0545

Director of Admissions
Seton Hill College
Greensburg, Pennsylvania
15601
412-834-2200

Director of Admissions
Tyler School of Art
Temple University
Beech and Penrose Avenues
Philadelphia, Pennsylvania
19126
215-224-7575

Director of Admissions
Westminster College
New Wilmington, Pennsylvania
16142
412-946-6710

Director of Admissions
Wilkes College
Wilkes-Barre, Pennsylvania
18703
717-824-4651

Additional Information

Executive Director
Pennsylvania Council on the Arts
503 North Front Street
Harrisburg, Pennsylvania
17101
717-787-6883

RHODE ISLAND

This state has two of the finer places to study crafts. When anyone talks about craft college, they talk about *Rhode Island School of Design*. This school does everything! Its craft offerings are wide and well-taught. In the Division of Fine Arts you can study textile design, light metals, ceramics, glassblowing, plus woodcarving and jewelry. The division has the goal to "promote the interrelationship of all creative activities."

Sculpture and ceramics are combined into one department "in the belief that the interrelation of the two areas is critical to the potential of the individual artist." A student selects his own program from the sculpture, ceramics, light metal and glass offerings. In the junior year the student concentrates in the major field.

The Department of Textile Design prepares students "to design for woven and printed fabrics and other media." The department offers everything in both weaves and prints.

A two-year Master of Fine Arts Degree is offered in ceramics, glassblowing and metalsmithing, among others. Also a Master of Arts in teaching.

Roger Williams College is another fine college for crafts. In this college there is a Fine Arts Division where an art major puts together a program of art history and studio art. The distribution of these courses is "based on the student's needs and interest, no specific art courses are required." Students at Roger Williams can take weaving, ceramics, stained glass and some general classes in metal.

This college is located on the shoreline, has a lovely small-town atmosphere and is only ninety minutes from Boston.

Addresses

Director of Admissions
Rhode Island School of Design
2 College Street
Providence, Rhode Island
02903
401-331-3507

Director of Admissions
Roger Williams College
Bristol, Rhode Island
02809
401-255-1000

Additional Information

Executive Director
Rhode Island State Council on
the Arts
4365 Post Road
East Greenwich, Rhode Island
02818
401-884-6410

SOUTH CAROLINA

Allen University has some jewelry and ceramics and a BA is possible, but the Art Department is limited. *Clemson University* offers only a few classes in ceramics. *Coker College* is a small, private place, a quiet and very nice college, where you can study ceramics, enameling, metals and weaving, or major in art. Check this college out. At the *University of South Carolina* there are about 10,000 students and a big BFA program with majors in jewelry, ceramics and textiles. You can obtain a BA in studio work, an intensive major. This is a very good school for crafts. An MFA is also awarded.

One other place to study crafts in the state, in an organized way, is the *Museum School of Art* in Greenville. It's a place to begin crafts only. Classes are offered in general crafts and ceramics, a certificate is given. Limited resources, but good instruction.

Addresses

Director of Admissions
Allen University
Harden and Taylor Streets
Columbia, South Carolina
29204
803-779-6430

Director of Admissions
Clemson University
Clemson, South Carolina
29631
803-656-3311

Director of Admissions
Coker College
Hartsville, South Carolina
29550
803-332-1381

Museum School of Art
106 DuPont Drive
Greenville, South Carolina
29607
803-233-0497

Director of Admissions
Art Department
University of South Carolina
Columbia, South Carolina
29208
803-777-0411

Additional Information

Executive Director
South Carolina Arts Commission
1001 Main Street
Columbia, South Carolina
29201
803-758-3442

SOUTH DAKOTA

The Art Department of *Northern State College* is housed in a new building with large studio space for all arts and crafts. Students here major in art, but they also specialize in one or two other areas; in crafts that could be ceramics, jewelry or weaving. Students take half their work in the Art Department. Pretty standard stuff. They place most of the graduates in teaching positions. It's about the only place in South Dakota where you can study crafts and get a degree, if you want a degree.

The *Civic Fine Arts Association* in Sioux Falls has a few craft classes for beginners. They are in jewelry, weaving and spinning. But taught mainly as hobbies. They can't hurt you, however.

Addresses

Raymond Shermoe, Director
Civic Fine Arts Association
318 South Main Avenue
Sioux Falls, South Dakota
57102
605-336-1167

Jim Gibson, Director of Art
Northern State College
Aberdeen, South Dakota
57401
605-622-2514

Additional Information

Executive Director
South Dakota State Fine Arts
Council
108 West 11th Street
Sioux Falls, South Dakota
57102
605-336-8050

TENNESSEE

Arrowmont School of Crafts is the Pi Beta Phi settlement school of the University of Tennessee. It began as a cottage industry and now is a school nationally known. They offer summer classes only, but soon will have year-round courses. New buildings have made this a beautiful campus set in seventy wooded acres. There is a new Loom House, a Ceramics House, all air-conditioned. Also the school has a library, auditorium and galleries. It's possible to obtain credit from the University of Tennessee or make other arrangements with schools.

At the *University of Tennessee* the craft courses are hidden away in the Home Economics Department, but the work is solid. Students can specialize in fiber, metal and clay. More than an adequate program.

In Clarksville *Austin Peay State University* gives an excellent professional crafts program. It is "designed for students planning a career in artistic handcraft productions, modified reproduction process in graphics, claywares, textiles and other fine art crafts." It offers all as a major. A small faculty, but one of the few places where you can work toward a degree as a production craftsman.

The *Memphis Academy of Art* is another fine private art school accredited by the National Association of Schools of Art. It awards a BFA and a certificate. Crafts taught are metal, pottery, textiles. A student is allowed to concentrate on a craft or take several. Excellent place.

Memphis State University offers a BFA degree in ceramics and textiles. The course work is standard. Not much imagination at the school. *Middle Tennessee State University* is not much of a place either. Craft courses are offered in quite a few areas, however, and a BFA is given. Small faculty, but lots of studio work and also lots of requirements. *Southern Missionary College* has a major in art; ceramics is the only craft offered.

Addresses

Director
Arrowmont School of Crafts
Box 567
Gatlinburg, Tennessee
37738
615-436-5860

Director of Admissions
Austin Peay State University
Clarksville, Tennessee
37040
615-648-7011

Director of Admissions
Memphis Academy of Art
Overton Park
Memphis, Tennessee
38112
901-272-1761

Director of Admissions
Memphis State University
Memphis, Tennessee
38111
901-321-1101

Director of Admissions
Middle Tennessee State University
Murfreesboro, Tennessee
37130
615-898-2300

Director of Admissions
Southern Missionary College
Collegedale, Tennessee
37315
615-396-2111

Director of Admissions
University of Tennessee
Knoxville, Tennessee
37916
615-974-0111

Individual Instruction

WOOD

Polly Page
P.O. Box 94
Pleasant Hill, Tennessee
38578

Additional Information

Executive Director
Tennessee Arts Commission
222 Capitol Hill Building
Nashville, Tennessee
37219
615-741-1701

TEXAS

Baylor University has a few courses: metal, silversmithing, ceramics, mostly for high school teachers. The *Craft Guild of Dallas* has classes in ceramics, weaving, silversmithing, bookbinding, jewelry. Courses are held for beginners, intermediate and advanced students. *East Texas State University* offers a BFA in jewelry and ceramics. This is mostly a fine arts college. They like sculpture work.

Fort Worth Art Center Museum School has bookbinding, ceramics, jewelry, weaving. Once-a-week classes and really only for beginners. *Hotsun Academy/110 in the Shade* is a small, private place that has classes in quite a few areas: metals, ceramics, wood and weaving. Mainly for beginners.

Mary Hardin Baylor College has a few classes in jewelry and ceramics. Nothing much. *McMurry College* is a small religious school controlled by the United Methodist Church. They have a couple of classes in ceramics. *North Texas State University* has a BFA in general crafts or specialization in ceramics, metalwork, jewelry, weaving and fabric design. An MFA is also possible. This is a huge school and the crafts program is extensive and well-designed.

Pan American University has a BA in metal, jewelry, ceramics, wood and weaving, but not much of a program of crafts emphasis at this place. *Sam Houston State University* is even worse, only ceramics and some textiles. This is very much a fine arts college. *San Antonio College* is a junior college and has courses in metal, silversmithing, jewelry and ceramics. Very general.

The *School of Art* of the Musem of Fine Arts in Houston is a fine arts school, but offers silversmithing, jewelry and ceramics. Strong crafts program given. Good place.

Southern Methodist University is a large, famous and very good college. They have a BFA and an MFA in ceramics, and ceramics is really the only strong area for crafts, though jewelry and weaving are taught. *Southwest Craft Center Creative Art School* is located in an 1851 former convent and is a lovely place to study crafts. They write, "This school is for the creative, contemporary and enthusiastic!" Crafts taught are: textiles, ceramics, wood, metals, jewelry. Extensive work and first-rate place.

Southwest Texas State University has jewelry, ceramics and textiles. They have a BA in art education; this place trains teachers. *Texas Christian University* offers a BFA and an MFA in metals and ceramics. This is a fine arts school; crafts come second. *Texas Tech University* gives a BFA in studio work, among other things. The major areas are ceramics and jewelry, also available are textiles and enameling. Program is structured but everything in crafts is here.

Texas Woman's University is a large place with a large program in art. It's possible to get a BA, BS and MA in ceramics, metals or weaving. New facilities and plenty of studio space and equipment. *University of Corpus Christi* has a small collection of courses: plastics, metal, ceramics, wood. Nothing much. The *University of Dallas* at Irving is a new Catholic-related college that has a BA, MA and MFA in ceramics. Good solid program in ceramics, not much else available.

The *University of Houston* is another large Texas school. They have a BFA in metal, jewelry and ceramics. Standard fare. At the *University of Texas* in Austin a BFA is given in plastics, enameling, metal, silversmithing and jewelry. Some general crafts also. Good place for students who are looking for a school that isn't dominated by ceramics.

The University of Texas at El Paso has a small program offering a BA in enameling, metal, silversmithing, jewelry, ceramics. Limited faculty and equipment. *West Texas State University* at Canyon has a BA and a BS degree. Enameling, metal, ceramics, jewelry are all taught. Small staff but adequate. *Wharton County Junior College* has a few courses, mostly ceramics. Nothing to write home about.

Addresses

Director of Admissions
Baylor University
Box 6367
Waco, Texas
76706
817-755-1011

Carol Campbell
Graft Guild of Dallas
Dallas Museum of Fine Arts
Fair Park
Dallas, Texas
75226
214-742-6421

Director of Admissions
East Texas State University
Commerce, Texas
75428
214-468-2562

Fort Worth Art Center
1309 Montgomery

Fort Worth, Texas
76107
817-738-9216

Director of Admissions
Mary Hardin Baylor College
Belton, Texas
76513
817-939-5811

Hotsun Academy/110 in the Shade
5119 East 7th Street
Austin, Texas
78702

Director of Admissions
McMurry College
P.O. Box 275
McMurry Station
Abilene, Texas
79605
915-692-4130

Addresses (Cont.)

Director of Admissions
North Texas State University
Box 13707
Benton, Texas
76203
817-788-2065

Director of Admissions
Pan American University
Edinburg, Texas
78539
512-383-3891

Director of Admissions
Sam Houston State University
Huntsville, Texas
77340
713-295-6211

Director of Admissions
San Antonio College
1300 San Pedro
San Antonio, Texas
78284
512-734-7311

Director of Admissions
School of Art
P.O. Box 6825
Houston, Texas
77005
713-526-1361

Director of Admissions
Southern Methodist University
Dallas, Texas
75222
214-692-2340

Director of Admissions
Southwest Craft Center
300 Augusta Street
San Antonio, Texas
78205
512-224-1848

Director of Admissions
Southwest Texas State University
San Marcus, Texas
78666
512-245-2111

Director of Admissions
Texas Christian University
Fort Worth, Texas
76129
817-926-2461

Director of Admissions
Texas Tech University
Box 4720
Lubbock, Texas
79409
806-742-0111

Director of Admissions
Texas Woman's University
Box 22909
Denton, Texas
76204
817-387-1322

Director of Admissions
University of Corpus Christi
P.O. Box 6010
Corpus Christi, Texas
78411
512-991-6810

Director of Admissions
University of Dallas
Irving, Texas
75060
214-251-1551

Director of Admissions
University of Houston
Cullen Boulevard
Houston, Texas
77004
713-749-1011

Director of Admissions
University of Texas
Austin, Texas
78712
512-471-3434

Director of Admissions
The University of Texas at
El Paso
El Paso, Texas
79968
915-747-5381

Director of Admissions
West Texas State University
Canyon, Texas
79015
806-656-0111

Director of Admissions
Wharton County Junior College
Boling Highway
Wharton, Texas
77488
713-532-4560

Additional Information

Executive Director
Texas Commission on the Arts
403 East 6th Street
Austin, Texas
78701
512-472-8237

UTAH

Brigham Young University has all the degrees offered—BA, BFA, MA, MFA—but their total program is small. Only jewelry, plastics and ceramics are taught. Dixie College teaches some ceramics and textile design. A very small Art Department. Southern Utah State College has a wide selection of craft courses and offers a straight BA. It's possible to concentrate in ceramics; small department here too.

The University of Utah, however, has a very good crafts program. A BFA is offered and an MFA. The school has a "strong emphasis on the basic courses." Drawing, design, jewelry, weaving, metals and woodcarving are taught. Requirements are many. There's a special design-craftsman and sculpture emphasis. It has an "extremely broad (base) in its orientation, but the slant of this Art Department, it should be remembered, is towards fine arts."

At Logan, Utah State University also has a BFA and MFA program. You can major in ceramics and metal. College has new and complete studios and equipment. A core curriculum is offered, then specialization. *Weber State College* has a half dozen craft courses, nothing concentrated or leading to a major.

One of the more interesting craft opportunities in the state is *Pioneer Craft House*. Most crafts are taught here. It's director is Mrs. A. L. Beeley, long an important member of the arts and crafts world of Salt Lake City. The place is mostly for beginners, but a good place to begin.

Addresses

Director of Admissions
Brigham Young University
Provo, Utah
84601
801-374-1211

Director of Admissions
Dixie College
225 South 700 East Street
George, Utah
84770
801-673-4811

Mrs. A. L. Beeley
Pioneer Craft House
3271 South 5th East
Salt Lake City, Utah
84106
801-467-6611

Director of Admissions
Southern Utah State College
Cedar City, Utah
84720
801-586-4411

Director of Admissions
University of Utah
309 Park Building
Salt Lake City, Utah
84112
801-581-7200

Director of Admissions
Utah State University
University Hill
Logan, Utah
84321
801-752-4100

Director of Admissions
Weber State College
3750 Harrison Boulevard
Ogden, Utah
84403
801-399-5941

Additional Information

Director
Utah State Institute of Fine Arts
609 East South Temple
Salt Lake City, Utah
84102
801-328-5895

VERMONT

The *Fletcher Farm Craft School* is sponsored by the society of Vermont craftsmen and it's a very fine place indeed. Classes, however, are only in the summer, arranged in two and three week periods. Courses in weaving, pottery, enameling, rosemaling (Norwegian folk art) and silver jewelry are taught among others. Classes are taught both in modern studios, an eighteenth-century New England farmhouse, an old sugarhouse, barns and a carriage house. Apply early, very popular place for the summer.

Another summer place in Vermont is with *Judy Fox* in Waitsfield. Judy teaches handweaving, spinning and dyeing. William Brauer is also there and teaches printmaking. "There" is a studio in rural Vermont, in a house over 100 years old. Judy writes, "It's peaceful but exciting learning experience." No room in the house for lodgers but students can camp on the meadows nearby.

To study—academically—crafts in Vermont, *Goddard*'s the place. This famous experimental college has lots of opportunities, thanks to Phil Homes who built the program and now runs it in the Chittenden Annex of the school. Also involved with the planning and building, particularly the glassblowing course, is John Bingham. Their program is (like the school) open, loose and highly individual. They have ceramics, weaving, glassblowing and a BA to earn. Look them up.

Addresses

Mrs. Harriet Clark Turnquist
Fletcher Farm Craft School
Chelsea, Vermont
05038
802-685-4863

Judy Fox
East Warren Road
Waitsfield, Vermont
05673
802-496-2402

Director of Admissions
Goddard College
Plainfield, Vermont
05667
802-454-8311

Additional Information

Executive Director
Vermont Council on the Arts
136 State Street
Montpelier, Vermont
05602
802-828-3291

VIRGINIA

Arts and Crafts Studio in Annandale offers a lot of hobby type courses, candle-making for one and something called paper tole. Nothing here for anyone serious. The *Hand Work Shop* is "a non-profit effort." It operates out of a restored 1840's house in Richmond. The goals are to "promote interest in hand crafts and arts . . . teaching these skills to children and adults." Classes are only for beginners and taught one night a week. Crafts taught pottery and weaving. Joan Koslan Schwartz runs the *Needle's Point Studio* out of her house in McLean. She's a rather well-known crafts woman and is considered by many as one "of the dynamic, infectiously enthusiastic and talented craftsmen" in the Washington area. She also conducts an educational working embroidery study tour to Scotland and England every summer. One of the few such ventures. Write for information about BEST (British Embroidery Study Tour) to her McLean address.

Longwood College has craft courses in enameling, jewelry and ceramics. This school has a sound approach to crafts. They write: "Creative learning and experimentation in the visual arts are encouraged. . . . Emphasis is placed on concept development . . . A foundation in art techniques is presented through experiences, studios, facilities, and faculty. The students are allowed to choose fields of specialization, form their own concepts, and develop individual methods." Longwood College is, unfortunately, only for women. A beautiful curriculum at a beautiful college in a beautiful town. Look into it!

The Department of Art at *Madison College* has a stiff curriculum preparing students who are seeking "careers as practicing artists, art historians, or as teachers of art on the secondary or elementary level." Most crafts are available. Students are required to take a long list of non-craft courses. This is a large school that leaves a lot to be desired.

Radford College is an odd place. It's a women's college run by men. Of the top eleven college administrators only four are women. They do offer a major in art and courses in ceramics, jewelry and enameling, but the school is out to produce teachers. A strict place. Not for the kinds of students I know.

The *University of Richmond* is made up of several colleges tied together on one campus. There's a men's college, a women's college, a law school, etc. A total of some 3,000 full-time undergraduates. A BA is offered in ceramics and students can concentrate in studio work for their degree. The ceramics is the only craft offered, some design courses, solid art foundation stuff but the possibilities and staff are limited.

Virginia State College is a predominantly black college that has some crafts: jewelry and ceramics, mainly introductory stuff. Nothing much. *Virginia Wesleyan College* is a Methodist-related place. A fairly extensive crafts program: weaving, ceramics, plastics, stitchery, but then some odd stuff like "cultural awareness." Good for elementary teachers, little for a serious crafts person.

The *Virginia Museum of Fine Arts* has some beginning craft classes: ceramics, weaving, also Raku, design, plus fine arts. They get part-time faculty from nearby colleges. All classes are held at the museum. This is a fine place to start in crafts, but that's all.

Huge *Virginia Commonwealth University* has the most extensive craft opportunities in the state. They offer a BFA and an MFA and they also have a BFA in plastics, one of the few such places. By far the best place to study crafts at any and all levels.

The new and small two-year community college of *Mountain Empire* in Big Gap has a very unique program in crafts production. It puts a strong emphasis on business practices for craftsmen. The primary objectives of the curriculum are for students to earn their living as producing craftsmen. One half of the student's time is spent taking courses in crafts, the rest in business-related areas. Worthwhile degree for someone wanting to go into the craft business. At the *Kiln Room* there's a possibility to work with Lee Magdanz, one of the better potters in the state. Located in Bristol, Virginia.

Addresses

Arts and Crafts Studio
Handcrafts Unlimited
7221 Little River Turnpike
Annandale, Virginia
22003
703-256-7550

Hand Work Shop
316 North 24th Street
Richmond, Virginia
23223
703-649-0674

The Kiln Room
Lee Magdanz
Bristol, Virginia
24201
703-669-8343

Director of Admissions
Longwood College
Farmville, Virginia
23901
703-392-4015

Director of Admissions
Madison College
Duke Fine Arts Center
Harrisonburg, Virginia
22801
703-433-6211

Director of Admissions
Mountain Empire Community
College
Drawer 700
Big Stone Gap, Virginia
24219
703-523-2400

Needle's Point Studio
1626 Macon Street
McLean, Virginia
22101
703-356-1615

Director of Admissions
Radford College
Radford, Virginia
24141
703-731-5000

Director of Admissions
University of Richmond
Richmond, Virginia
23173
703-285-6000

Director of Admissions
Virginia Commonwealth
University
901 West Franklin
Richmond, Virginia
23220
703-770-0000

Virginia Museum of Fine Arts
Boulevard and Grove Avenues
Richmond, Virginia
23221
703-770-6344

Director of Admissions
Virginia State College
Box 26
Petersburg, Virginia
23803
703-526-5111

Director of Admissions
Virginia Wesleyan College
Wesleyan Drive
Norfolk, Virginia
23502
703-464-6291

Additional Information

Executive Director
Virginia Commission on the Arts
Ninth Street Office Building
Richmond, Virginia
23219
703-770-4492

VIRGIN ISLANDS

Crafts are taught in a limited way on the islands. On St. Croix there is a *School of the Arts* that's in its third year. It is directed by Dorothy Raedler and has classes in Caribbean crafts using wood, seeds, clay and bamboo. Also jewelry, wood sculpture, stitchery. Classes are taught in a local high school.

Conrad Knowles has a ceramics school at the Estate Concordia. Classes are for both children and adults. The school/shop is called *Conrad's Ceramics* and besides usual techniques, he teaches Raku production.

There has been talk on St. Croix of starting an arts center called Genesis at the old Peace Corps training center near Frederiksted. The American Crafts Council was rumored to be involved but nothing has come of that so far.

Addresses

Conrad's Ceramics
Conrad Knowles
57 Hill Street
Christiansted, St. Croix
Virgin Islands
00820

St. Croix School of the Arts
Box 1086
Christiansted, St. Croix
Virgin Islands
00820
809-773-3767

Additional Information

Virgin Island Council on the Arts
Caravelle Arcade
Christiansted, St. Croix
Virgin Islands
00820
809-773-3075

WASHINGTON

Bellevue Community College has weaving, several courses, but not all that worthwhile. *Skagit Valley College* is a junior college offering beginning courses in jewelry, ceramics, textile design. *Green River Community College* is the same. They have design classes and ceramics; it's also possible to get a course or two in welding. *Wenatchee Valley College* has just jewelry, ceramics, metal and some wood. Limited to say the least. *Shoreline Community College* has ceramics only. *Spokane Falls Community College* has, however, a good creative arts program. Courses in jewelry, ceramics and metals. Good beginner place.

Central Washington State College has more courses: glassblowing, jewelry, ceramics, woodworking. They train teachers. Also a graduate school; they, too, train teachers. *Eastern Washington State College* is a large state place and their craft offerings are many but scattered, no degrees offered. They have new equipment, but most courses are limited to beginner's stuff. You can do much better elsewhere. *Western Washington State College* has it worse. There are jewelry, ceramics and some weaving.

Lower Columbia College has just ceramics and that's not what you want. *Pacific Lutheran University* is a pretty good place to begin. They write, "No formal entrance standards are maintained by the Department (Art). Students are encouraged to select courses relating to their interests as early as possible in order to reasonably determine aptitude and suitability for the area of study." They have a BFA degree and offer courses in ceramics, glassblowing and metals. Also lots of history and theory.

University of Puget Sound has a BA and a BFA in ceramics. Jewelry is also offered. But ceramics is it at this place! The *University of Washington* has a BA and also an MFA in metal, silversmithing, jewelry and ceramics. This is a school with a very large Art Department and courses are opened to the whole campus. It trains teachers as well as professionals for careers in graphics and plastic arts. You can get a solid base in crafts at this place. *Whitworth College* just has general crafts, some jewelry. It's a small, church-related school and harmless. It is a college, they write, "with Jesus Christ as a theme."

The *Cornish School of Allied Arts* is a small private school that teaches art, ballet and music. Their craft courses are limited to pottery and jewelry. Not very advanced. In Bellevue an excellent place for pottery is *Crockery Pottery*. It's a wheel-craft school and has small classes (seven students) that run for eight one-hour sessions for two months. They are excellent teachers and the place is a good location to start. Inexpensive, too.

The *Factory of Visual Arts* is just a very fine place. Period. It has a good reputation and deserves it. The school opened in 1968, housed in a large, old building and committed to "serious art experiences." The Factory offers a complete education in art at the college level on a full-time or a part-time basis. Five programs are offered. Students wanting to obtain a degree from the Factory need to spend three years at the school. All crafts are taught by a top-notch faculty. A very fine place.

Pottery Northwest, also in Seattle, is in many ways a better place for the potter. This is an organization of potters from the Northwest who needed space work so they joined together. They have the third floor—some 6,700 square feet—of a building which is fully equipped with five gas kilns, three electric kilns, a clay mixer, complete glazing facilities and twenty wheels. The workshop is open to any potter. Classes are taught by potters holding at least MFA degrees in ceramics. Classes run three-hours, once a week for one quarter. Beginners also have unlimited access to pottery facilities and can work side by side with professional potters. That alone is worth going to this school for.

Addresses

Director of Admissions
Bellevue Community College
9923 S.E. Bellevue Place
Bellevue, Washington
98004
206-641-0111

Director of Admissions
Central Washington State College
Ellensburg, Washington
98926
509-963-1111

Director of Admissions
Cornish School of Allied Arts
710 East Roy Street
Seattle, Washington
98102
206-323-1400

Director of Admissions
Crockery Pottery
826—102nd N.E.
Bellevue, Washington
98004
206-454-1250

Addresses (Cont.)

Director of Admissions
Eastern Washington State College
Cheney, Washington
99004
509-359-2398

The Factory of Visual Arts
5041 Roosevelt Way
Seattle, Washington
98155
206-632-8177

Director of Admissions
Green River Community College
12401 Southeast 320th
Auburn, Washington
98002
206-833-9111

Director of Admissions
Lower Columbia College
Longview, Washington
98632
206-425-6500

Director of Admissions
Pacific Lutheran University
P.O. Box 2068
Tacoma, Washington
98447
206-531-6900

Pottery Northwest
305 Harrison Street
Seattle, Washington
98109
206-624-9504

Director of Admissions
Shoreline Community College
Richmond Beach, Washington
98160
206-546-4101

Director of Admissions
Skagit Valley College
2405 College

Mount Vernon, Washington
98273
206-424-1031

Director of Admissions
Spokane Falls Community College
West 3410 Fort George Wright
Drive
Spokane, Washington
99204
509-456-6100

Director of Admissions
University of Puget Sound
1500 North Warner
Tacoma, Washington
98416
206-759-3531

Director of Admissions
University of Washington
Seattle, Washington
98195
206-543-0646

Director of Admissions
Wenatchee Valley College
1300 Fifth Street
Wenatchee, Washington
98801
509-663-5126

Director of Admissions
Western Washington State College
Bellingham, Washington
98225
206-676-3000

Director of Admissions
Whitworth College
Spokane, Washington
99218
509-489-3550

Individual Instruction

SPRANG, WEAVING

Hella Skowronski
9923 South East Bellevue Place
Bellevue, Washington
98004
206-454-1589

WEAVING

Lillian Hjert
2635 29th Avenue West
Seattle, Washington
98199
206-282-5114

Additional Information

Northwest Designer Craftsmen
Louella Simpson
1440 S.W. 158th Street
Seattle, Washington
98102

Executive Director
Washington State Arts Commission
4800 Capitol Boulevard
Olympia, Washington
98504
206-753-3860

WEST VIRGINIA

The *Oglebay Institute* is the most important of the non-academic places for crafts in West Virginia. Oglebay offers art and craft courses for "leisure-time education during spring, fall and winter." They also have some workshops in sewing, candle-making, that sort of stuff. The place is mostly artsy-craftsy. The *Huntington Galleries* has some adult classes in ceramics and also new classes in "creative needlepoint." These classes meet once a week in the evening, mostly for people looking for hobbies. There are some day classes in weaving, also only once a week.

Salem College has a rather special program in the study of the arts, crafts, lore, music and the way of life in West Virginia and the Appalachians at the time of settlement. Students can get instruction in spinning and weaving, basketweaving and chair bottoms, pottery, blacksmith and metal work. For those interested in this area of crafts, this is something to look into.

Glenville State College has a pretty good program, very good for West Virginia. A student can work toward a BA in education or study crafts alone. Faculty is very small, however. One good potter, Charles Scott. Weaving is also possible, but again limited. The college is located in a quiet town, that's some advantage. Straight students.

  Marshall University in Huntington is a bigger school but even less is offered in crafts. There are ceramics, metal and some art appreciation classes, but that's all. The school is not worth it for crafts. At *West Virginia College* you can earn a BA and/or a BS but here all that's offered is ceramics and weaving. Lots of requirements. Avoid.

Addresses

Director of Admissions
Glenville State College
Glenville, West Virginia
26351
304-462-7361

Director of Admissions
The Heritage Arts
Salem College
Salem, West Virginia
26426
304-782-5011

Director of Admissions
Huntington Galleries
Park Hills
Huntington, West Virginia
25701
304-522-7373

Director of Admissions
Marshall University
Huntington, West Virginia
25701
304-696-3170

Director of Admissions
Oglebay Institute
841½ National Road
Wheeling, West Virginia
26003
304-242-4200

Director of Admissions
West Virginia College
Institute, West Virginia
25112
304-766-3000

Additional Information

West Virginia Arts Council
State Office Building 6
1900 Washington Street, East
Charleston, West Virginia
25305
304-348-3711

WISCONSIN

Alverno College has just ceramics and weaving and a few other general introduction courses. Nothing much. *Cardinal Stritch College* trains teachers. They have ceramics, metals, jewelry. Good place for foundation work, but college on the whole isn't interesting. *Carroll College* has some classes: jewelry, ceramics and textiles. Very limited. *Edgewood College* offers a few courses in ceramics; this is a fine arts place.

Marian College of Fond Du Luc has all crafts offered and a degree. It's another Catholic college. They have a concentration in metal and ceramics taken after a general introduction to arts and crafts. Basic but good courses here. *Milkwaukee Area Technical College* has crafts in their Graphic and Applied Arts Division. The areas are: fiber, clay, metal and plastics. The emphasis of the course is "on the combining of creative design, proper techniques, and fine craftsmanship." Excellent place to start work in crafts. You can learn a lot at this school.

Mount Mary College, a women's school, has a big Art Department that trains teachers, fashion designers and prepares students for graduate study. They do offer courses in most crafts and students can concentrate. Design segment is the best bet. *St. Norbert College* offers a BFA and metals and ceramics are taught, but this is a fine arts place. *Stout State University* trains teachers and they have courses in ceramics and metals, but limited. Go elsewhere in this state.

The *University of Wisconsin at Eau Claire* has a BFA with studio concentration in either ceramics, fibers, metals. Design and fine arts courses also required. This is mainly a fine arts campus. At *Green Bay* the *University of Wisconsin* is much more limited in crafts. They have a BA in metal, jewelry, ceramics and wood. This is in their visual arts option, it qualifies as a co-major. The *University of Wisconsin-La Crosse* has just jewelry and ceramics.

The *Madison* campus of the *University of Wisconsin* has one of the best craft opportunities in the state. They offer BAs, MSs and MFAs in glassblowing, wood, ceramics and metals. A huge campus and a very good place to go to school. Another fine branch of the *University of Wisconsin* is in *Milwaukee*. They offer a BFA, MA and MFA in all major crafts. A core curriculum is taken, then concentration in upper levels. Fine facilities and a fine institution. The School of Fine Arts is a lively place. At *Oshkosh* the *University of Wisconsin* has only a few courses: metals, ceramics, weaving. Nothing really worthwhile.

The *University of Wisconsin-Platteville* has some craft courses in the Department of Art: ceramics and jewelry. Nothing here. At *Stevens Point* there's some design and studio courses in ceramics, textiles, metal and wood. Lots of history. Serious studies. *University of Wisconsin-Superior* has a BFA in the major crafts but their program is not impressive; it's mostly a fine arts and art history place. At *Whitewater* the *University of Wisconsin* has a BA and a BS in education. Limited crafts and lots of requirements.

Viterbo College is a coeducational Catholic college, trains teachers, is mostly a fine arts place. They have ceramics and weaving.

Addresses

Director of Admissions
Alverno College
3401 South 39th Street
Milwaukee, Wisconsin
53215
414-671-5400

Director of Admissions
Cardinal Stritch College
6801 North Yates Road
Milwaukee, Wisconsin
53217
414-352-5400

Director of Admissions
Carroll College
Waukesha, Wisconsin
53186
414-547-1211

Director of Admissions
Edgewood College
855 Woodrow Street
Madison, Wisconsin
53711
608-257-4861

Director of Admissions
Marian College of Fond Du Lac
45 National Avenue
Fond Du Lac, Wisconsin
54935
414-921-3900

Director of Admissions
Milwaukee Area Technical College
1015 North Sixth Street
Milwaukee, Wisconsin
53303
414-278-6600

Director of Admissions
Mount Mary College
2900 Menomonie River Parkway
Milwaukee, Wisconsin
53222
414-258-4810

Director of Admissions
St. Norbert College
West De Pere
Green Bay, Wisconsin
54178
414-336-3181

Director of Admissions
Stout State University
Menomonie, Wisconsin
54751
715-232-0123

Director of Admissions
University of Wisconsin
Eau Claire, Wisconsin
54701
715-836-0123

Director of Admissions
University of Wisconsin
120 University Circle
Green Bay, Wisconsin
54302
414-465-2111

Director of Admissions
University of Wisconsin
La Crosse, Wisconsin
54601
608-785-1800

Director of Admissions
University of Wisconsin
Madison, Wisconsin
53706
608-262-3961

Director of Admissions
University of Wisconsin
Milwaukee, Wisconsin
53201
414-963-4572

Director of Admissions
University of Wisconsin
Oshkosh, Wisconsin
54901
414-424-0202

Director of Admissions
University of Wisconsin
Platteville, Wisconsin
53818
608-342-1125

Director of Admissions
University of Wisconsin
Stevens Point, Wisconsin
54481
715-346-2669

Director of Admissions
University of Wisconsin
Superior, Wisconsin
54880
715-392-8101

Director of Admissions
University of Wisconsin
Baker Hall
Whitewater, Wisconsin
53190
414-472-1440

Director of Admissions
Viterbo College
815 South Ninth Street
LaCrosse, Wisconsin
54601
608-783-3450

Additional Information

Executive Director
Wisconsin Arts Council
P.O. Box 3356
Madison, Wisconsin
53704
608-266-0190

WYOMING

Northwest Community College has some craft courses in jewelry and ceramics. Not very much.

Addresses

Director of Admissions
Northwest Community College
Powell, Wyoming
82435
307-754-5151

Additional Information

Executive Director
Wyoming Council on the Arts
P.O. Box 3033
Casper, Wyoming
82601
307-265-5434

PART III

DIRECTORY OF NATIONAL ASSOCIATION OF SCHOOLS OF ART

Accredited schools offering programs intended to be professional, and normally leading to the BFA and MFA and similar professional degrees.

Institution (by state)	ALABAMA	CALIFORNIA		
	Auburn University Department of Art	Art Center College of Design	California College of Arts and Crafts	California Institute of the Arts (Chouinard Art School)
Mailing Address	Auburn, Alabama 36830	5353 West 3rd Street Los Angeles, California 90020	5212 Broadway Oakland, California 94618	24700 McBean Parkway Valencia, California 91355
Telephone	(205) 826-4373	(213) 938-5166	(415) 653-8118	(805) 255-1050
Major Programs	Advertising design and illustration, fashion	Communications arts, film, advertising design, graphics,	Painting, sculpture, ceramics, metal arts, graphic design,	School of art, school of design.

	ALABAMA	**CALIFORNIA**		
Major Programs (cont.)	illustration, drawing, painting and printmaking.	photography, illustration, fashion illustration, package design, industrial design, environmental design, product design, transportation design, interior space design, fine arts.	textile arts, interior design, industrial design, printmaking, illustration, teacher education, film, photography, television.	
Summer Programs	12 Weeks: Full Program	Regular Trimester (full term program)	6 Weeks: Full Program	3 Terms: a) 10 Weeks b) 10 Weeks c) 10 Weeks d) Summer Sessions
Degree/ Certificate	BFA—4 years MFA—2 years	BFA, BS—8 terms MFA, MS—4 terms	BFA—4 years MFA—1½-2 years	BFA—4 years MFA—2 years Certificate— 2 years
			CONNECTICUT	**GEORGIA**
Institution (by state)	**Otis Art Institute of the Los Angeles County**	**San Francisco Art Institute** formerly the California School of Fine Arts	**Hartford Art School** University of Hartford	**Atlanta School of Art**
Mailing Address	2401 Wilshire Blvd. Los Angeles, California 90057	800 Chestnut Street San Francisco, California 94133	200 Bloomfield Avenue West Hartford, Connecticut 06117	1280 Peachtree Street NE Atlanta, Georgia 30309

Telephone	(213) 387-5288	(415) 771-7020	(203) 523-4811	(404) 892-3600
Major Programs	Drawing, design, painting, sculpture, ceramics, printmaking.	Painting, sculpture/ ceramics, photography, printmaking, humanities, film-making.	Painting, sculpture, graphic arts, advertising design, art education, photography, film, TV, ceramics.	Graphic design, painting, printmaking, sculpture.
Summer Programs	6 Weeks: Full Program	3 Four-Week Summer Sessions: Photography, painting, sculpture/ ceramics, printmaking, film-making.	2 Six Weeks, 8 Weeks: Drawing, paint- ing, sculpture, ceramics, pho- tography, print- making, art education.	8 Weeks: Fine Arts, design.
Degree/ Certificate	BFA—2 years residence—(2 years college prereq.) MFA—2 years	BFA—4 years MFA—1½ years	BFA—4 years BS Art Ed—4 years MFA M Art Ed	BFA—4 years

ILLINOIS

Institution (by state)	**Institute of Design, Illinois Institute of Technology**	**School of the Art Institute of Chicago**	**Northern Illinois University** Department of Art	**University of Illinois** Department of Art
Mailing Address	3360 South State Street Chicago, Illinois 60616	Michigan Ave- nue at Adams Street Chicago, Illinois 60603	DeKalb, Illinois 60115	Champaign, Illinois 61820

ILLINOIS

Telephone	(312) 225-9600 Ext 471	(312) 236-7080	(815) 753-1473	(217) 333-0855
Major Programs	Visual communication, product design, photography, color photography, design methodology, cinematography, film animation.	Design/crafts, environmental design, fashion design, film-making, painting, photography, printmaking, sculpture, teacher education, visual communications.	Drawing, painting, printmaking, sculpture, textiles, metalwork and jewelry, interior/environmental design, comprehensive design, advertising and graphic design, industrial design, ceramics, art history, art education, photography. Foreign study programs.	Art education, art history, crafts, graphic design, industrial design, painting, printmaking, sculpture, medical art.
Summer Programs	8 Weeks: Visual, education, printmaking.	8 Weeks: Advanced ceramics workshop, design/crafts, film-making, history of art, painting, photography, printmaking, sculpture, teacher education, weaving.	8 Weeks: All Areas	8 Weeks: Full Program
Degree/ Certificate	BS—4 years in: Design MS—1-2 years in: Visual Design, Product Design, Photography, Visual Education.	BFA—4 years MFA—2 years	BS, BA, BFA, MS, MA, MFA	BFA—4 years MA Art Ed and Art Hist —1 year MFA—2 years DEd PhD Art Hist

	INDIANA	KANSAS	MARYLAND	MASSA-CHUSETTS
Institution (by state)	Herron School of Art, Indiana University—Purdue University at Indianapolis	University of Kansas Visual Arts Division	The Maryland Institute College of Art	Massachusetts College of Art
Mailing Address	1701 N. Pennsylvania St. Indianapolis, Indiana 46202	Lawrence, Kansas 66044	1300 Mt. Royal Avenue Baltimore, Maryland 21217	Brookline and Longwood Avenues Boston, Massachusetts 02215
Telephone	(317) 923-3651	(913) 864-4401	(301) 669-9200	(617) 731-2340
Major Programs	Painting, sculpture, printmaking, graphic design, art education.	Design, drawing, painting, industrial design, illustration, graphic design, printmaking, sculpture, ceramics, jewelry and silversmithing, weaving, teacher education, art history, occupational therapy, theater design.	Painting, sculpture, graphic design, illustration, art teacher education, interior design, fashion design, photography-film, designer-craftsman.	Art education, painting, printmaking, sculpture, crafts, photography, industrial design, fashion design, graphic design media, illustration.
Summer Programs	8 Weeks	8 Weeks: Design, drawing, painting, jewelry and silversmithing, weaving.	6 Weeks: Full Program	6 Weeks: Graduate and Undergraduate Art Education, Fine Arts and Design.

	INDIANA	KANSAS	MARYLAND	MASSA-CHUSETTS
Degree/ Certificate	BFA—4 years BAE—4 years	BFA—4 years BS—4 years MFA—2 years	BFA—4 years MFA—2 years Diploma—3 years	BSEd—4 years BFA—4 years MSEd

			MICHIGAN
Institution (by state)	School of the Museum of Fine Arts	School of the Worcester Art Museum	Cranbrook Academy of Art
Mailing Address	230 The Fenway Boston, Massachusetts 02115	55 Salisbury Street Worcester, Massachusetts 01608	Bloomfield Hills, Michigan 48103
Telephone	(617) 267-9300	(617) 752-4678	(313) 644-1600
Major Programs	Painting, sculpture, drawing, graphic arts and design, jewelry and metalsmithing, ceramics, photography, film.	Drawing and painting, visual design, sculpture, graphics, advertising art, photography.	Architecture, ceramics, design, metalsmithing, painting and drawing, printmaking, sculpture, fabric design.
Summer Programs	6 Weeks Incoming Students	Summer Program	No Summer Program
Degree/ Certificate	BFA—4 years (with Tufts University) BS-Ed—4½ years (with Tufts University) MFA—2 years (with Tufts University) Diploma—4 years Grad Cert—1 year	BA (with Clark University) 2 years beyond Cert. Program Cert—3 years BFA (Evening College)	BFA—2 years residence (2 years college prereq.) MFA—2 years

Institution (by state)	University of Michigan College of Architecture and Design Department of Art	MINNESOTA Minneapolis College of Art and Design	MISSOURI Kansas City Art Institute	Washington University School of Fine Arts
Mailing Address	Ann Arbor, Michigan 48104	200 East 25th Street Minneapolis, Minnesota 55404	4415 Warwick Blvd. Kansas City, Missouri 64111	St. Louis, Missouri 63130
Telephone	(313) 764-0397	(612) 339-8905	(816) 561-4852	(314) 863-0100
Major Programs	Painting, sculpture, printmaking, photography, ceramics, design, interior design, medical-scientific illustration (grad prog) (art ed certification optional).	Video and cinema, photo, painting, sculpture, printmaking, graphic design, fashion design, drawing.	Ceramics, graphic design, industrial design, photography/ cinematography, painting and printmaking, sculpture.	Painting, sculpture, printmaking, multi-media, graphic communication, fashion design, metalsmithing, ceramics, art teacher education, photography.
Summer Programs	6 Weeks: Art Education and Special Study	4-8 Weeks: Workshops, High School and Art Teachers Special Courses	8 Weeks: Fine Arts Design	Two 4½ Week sessions Nine Week day session Eight Week

	MINNESOTA	MISSOURI	
Summer Programs (cont.)			evening session: Drawing, painting, sculpture, print-making, ceramics, photography.
Degree/ Certificate	BS—4 years MA—1 year MFA—2 years BFA—4 years MS Med Ill.—2½ years	BFA—4 years	BFA—4 years	BFA—4 years MAT—1 year and 1 summer session MFA—2 years MA Ed—1–2 years

NEW YORK

Institution (by state)	**Cooper Union School of Art and Architecture**	**Parsons School of Design** A division of The New School	**Pratt Institute School of Art and Design**	**Rochester Institute of Technology** College of Fine and Applied Arts
Mailing Address	Cooper Square New York, New York 10003	66 West 12th Street New York, New York 10011	200 Grand Avenue Brooklyn, New York 11205	One Lomb Memorial Dr. Rochester, New York 14623
Telephone	(212) 254-6300	(212) 759-2214	(212) 622-2200	(716) 464-2644

Major Programs	Art and architecture	Communications design, environmental design, fashion design, fashion illustration, interior design, product design, urban design, general illustration.	Art education, communications design, environmental and interior design, fashion design, fashion visuals, film and photography, industrial design, painting and drawing, printmaking, sculpture and ceramics, art therapy (graduate level), package design (graduate level)	Communications design, industrial and environmental design, painting, printmaking, ceramics, metalcraft and jewelry, weaving and textile design, woodworking and furniture design, art education (graduate level)
Summer Programs	No Summer Program	6 Weeks: Pre-College Liberal Arts Program for BFA Candidates	12 Weeks: Undergraduate 6 Weeks Graduate Art Ed. Graduate Fine Arts	5–10 Weeks: Selected Arts and Crafts Graduate and Undergraduate
Degree/ Certificate	BFA—4 years B Arch—5 years Certificate—4 years	BFA—4 years or 3 years 3 Summers certificate—3 years	BFA—4 years BID—4 years MSAE—1 year MID—2 years MFA—2 years MSPD—2 years MSInt—1½ years	BFA—4 years MFA—2 years MST Art Ed —1 year Pre-College
Institution (by state)	**State University of New York** Division of Art and Design at Alfred University		**State University of New York at Buffalo** Department of Art	**Syracuse University** School of Art

NEW YORK

Mailing Address	Alfred, New York 14802	4240 Ridge Lea Campus Amherst, New York 14226	Lowe Art Center 309 University Place Syracuse, New York 13210
Telephone	(607) 587-8111 Ext 42	(716) 831-1251	(315) 476-5541 Ext 2611

Major Programs	Ceramics, design, glass, painting, printmaking, sculpture, teacher certification.	Communications design, painting, photography, printmaking, art education, art history.	Painting, design, sculpture, art education, industrial design, advertising, illustration, fabric design, ceramics, silversmithing, weaving, interior design, printmaking, art history, fashion illustration, costume design, muscology.
Summer Programs	6 Weeks: Full Program Graduate and Undergraduate	3–6 Weeks: Fine Arts, Art History	6 Weeks: Art Education, 5 Weeks Pre-College, Full Program
Degree/ Certificate	BFA—4 years MFA—2-3 years	BA Art Hist—4 years BA Studio—4 years BFA—4 years MFA—2 years MA— (Humanities) EdM— (Art Education)	BFA—4 years BID—5 years MID—2 years MFA—2 years

NORTH CAROLINA

OHIO

Institution (by state)	School of Art, East Carolina University	University of North Carolina at Chapel Hill Department of Art	Art Academy of Cincinnati	Cleveland Institute of Art

Mailing Address	PO Box 2704 Greenville, North Carolina 27834	Ackland Art Center Chapel Hill, North Carolina 27514	Eden Park Cincinnati, Ohio 45202	11141 East Blvd. Cleveland, Ohio 44106
Telephone	(919) 758-6665	(919) 933-2016	(513) 721-5205	(216) 421-4322
Major Programs	Art education, painting, sculpture, printmaking, ceramics, commercial art, interior design, design, art history.	Painting, sculpture, printmaking, art history, art education.	Painting, sculpture, advertising design, illustration, graphic arts, photography. History of the arts, 4 years.	Painting, sculpture, printmaking, graphic design, industrial design, ceramics, jewelry and silversmithing, weaving and textile design, teacher training, photography.
Summer Programs	2–6 Weeks	15 Weeks	8 Weeks: Fine Arts	6 Weeks: Graduate and Undergraduate study
Degree/ Certificate	BFA—4 years BS Art Ed—4 years AB Art Hist—4 years AB Art—4 years MA, MA Art Ed—1 year MFA—2 years	AB—4 years BFA—4 years MA Art Hist—2 years MFA Painting & Sculpture—2 years PhD Art History	Certificate—4 years BS-FA & Design—5 years (with University of Cincinnati)	BFA—5 years BS Ed—4 years MS Ed—5 years (with Case Western Reserve U)

Institution (by state)	Kent State University School of Art	School of the Dayton Art Institute	University of Cincinnati College of De-sign, Architecture and Art	Museum Art School
Mailing Address	Kent, Ohio 44240	Forest and Riverview Avenues Dayton, Ohio 45401	Cincinnati, Ohio 45221	Park Avenue at Madison, SW Portland, Oregon 97205
Telephone	(216) 672-2192	(513) 223-1242	(513) 475-4933	(503) 226-4391
Major Programs	Art history, advertising, design, art education, painting, sculpture, printmaking, design and crafts, industrial design, cinematography.	Ceramics, design correlations, graphic design, illustration, painting, photography, printmaking, sculpture.	Graphic design, fashion design, industrial design, interior design, fine arts, art history, art education. Operates on the co-operative or work study systems as well as the traditional full-time plan. Graduate programs in fine arts, art history and art education.	Painting, sculpture, ceramics, advertising design, printmaking.
Summer Programs	Summer Program 10 Weeks in two 5 Week Sessions Blossom-Kent	6 Weeks: Full Program	Art Education Majors Summer School Studios Electives in all other regular	6 Weeks: Painting, Ceramics

Summer Programs (cont.)	Art Program: A special program for Graduate Students and Professionals —6 Weeks		academic & professional art areas
Degree/ Certificate	BA—4 years BS—4 years BFA—4 years MA—1 year MFA—2 years	Diploma—4 years BFA—5 years Other degrees with U. of Dayton, Wright State U.	BS—5 years BFA Fine Arts Art Ed—4 years BA Art Hist—4 years MFA—2 years MA—Art Ed— 1 year MA Art Hist— 1 year	BFA—4 years BA—5 years (Affiliated with Reed College)

PENNSYLVANIA

Institution (by state)	**Carnegie-Mellon University** College of Fine Arts	**Moore College of Art**	**Philadelphia College of Art**	**Tyler School of Art** Temple University
Mailing Address	Schenley Park Pittsburgh, Pennsylvania 15213	20th and Race Streets Philadelphia, Pennsylvania 19103	Broad and Pine Streets Philadelphia, Pennsylvania 19102	Beech and Penrose Avenues Philadelphia, Pennsylvania 19126
Telephone	(412) 621-2600 Ext 427	(215) 568-4515	(215) 546-0545	(215) 224-7575
Major Programs	Painting, sculpture, industrial	Art education, advertising art, fashion design,	Art education, craft, environmental design,	Painting, printmaking,

PENNSYL-VANIA

Major Programs (cont.)	design, graphic arts, stage design,* art education, architecture.*	fashion illustration, interior design, painting, illustration, textile arts, photography, ceramic design, printmaking, jewelry and metalsmithing, sculpture.	fibres, graphic design, illustration, industrial design, painting, photography and film, printmaking, sculpture.	sculpture, graphic design, ceramics, metalsmithing, weaving, teacher certification program. One year Rome study.
Summer Programs	6 Weeks: Pre-College Programs** Regular Program	Summer Program High School Regular College Jr. High School College Preparatory	4 Weeks: Pre-College	6 Weeks: Full Program Philadelphia and Rome
Degree/ Certificate	BFA—4 years MFA M Arch* DA (Education) * Accredited, but not by NASA ** No accreditation sought	BSAE—4 years BFA—4 years	BFA—4 years BS—4 years MA Art Ed—1 year M Des in Community Design—2 years	BFA, BA through the College of Liberal Arts MFA, M Ed through the College of Education

	RHODE ISLAND	TENNESSEE	TEXAS
Institution (by state)	**Rhode Island School of Design**	**Memphis Academy of Arts**	**University of Texas** College of Fine Arts Department of Art
Mailing Address	Providence, Rhode Island 02903	Overton Park Memphis, Tennessee 38112	23rd and San Jacinto Austin, Texas 78712

Telephone	(401) 331-3507	(901) 272-1761	(512) 471-3365

Major Programs	Painting, communications design, graphic design, sculpture, ceramics, photography, architecture, landscape architecture, interior architecture, industrial design, film-making, apparel design, textile design, art education, liberal arts.	Painting, sculpture, advertising design, interior design, printmaking, photography, metal arts, pottery, textiles.	Painting, sculpture, printmaking, ceramics, photography, advertising design, metal and jewelry design, art education, history of art.
Summer Programs	6 Weeks: Required of transfer entrants	6 Weeks: Crafts emphasis	12 Weeks: Full Program
Degree/ Certificate	BFA—4 years B Arch—5 years B Land Arch—5 years B Ind Des—5 years B Int Arch—5 years MAT Art Ed—1 year MA Art Ed—1 year MFA—2 years	BFA—4 years Certificate—4 years	BFA—4 years BS—4 years MFA—1 year MA Art Hist—1 year
	VIRGINIA	**WASHINGTON**	**WISCONSIN**
Institution (by state)	**Virginia Commonwealth University** School of the Arts	**University of Washington** School of Art	**Layton School of Art and Design**
Mailing Address	901 West Franklin Richmond, Virginia 23220	Seattle, Washington 98105	4650 North Port Washington Road Milwaukee, Wisconsin 53212

	VIRGINIA	WASHINGTON	WISCONSIN
Telephone	(703) 770-7262	(206) 543-0970	(414) 962-0215
Major Programs	Art education, art history, communication arts and design, crafts, fashion design, interior design, photography, painting and printmaking, sculpture, theatre design, museum administration.	Painting, sculpture, printmaking, ceramics, industrial design, graphic design, interior design, metal design, art education, general art, art history.	Visual communications, illustration, industrial design, interior design, painting, sculpture, printmaking.
Summer Programs	3 Week, Pre; 6 Week, Regular; 3 Week, Post; Special Workshops and Seminars 9 Week, Reg.	9 Weeks	Summer Program: Fine Arts Design
Degree/ Certificate	BFA—8 terms MFA—4 terms MA—3 terms MAE—3 terms	BA—4 years BFA—5 years MFA—2 years MA—Art History MAT—Art Education PhD—Art History	BFA—4 years Diploma—4 years

Schools offering major studies in art normally leading to the BA and MA and similar degrees.

	CALIFORNIA	LOUISIANA	MICHIGAN
Institution (by state)	**California State College, Long Beach** Department of Art	**Tulane University, Newcomb College** Department of Art	**Western Michigan University** Art Department

Mailing Address	6101 East 7th Street Long Beach, California 90801	1229 Broadway New Orleans, Louisiana 70118	Kalamazoo, Michigan 49001
Telephone	(213) 433-4376	(504) 865-7711	(616) 383-1858
Major Programs	Art history, drawing and painting, printmaking, sculpture, illustration, graphic design, interior design, industrial design, textile design, ceramics, metalsmithing and jewelry, theatre design, general crafts.	Art history, ceramics, drawing, painting, printmaking, sculpture.	Painting, sculpture, printmaking, graphic design, ceramics, jewelry and metalsmithing, weaving and textile design, teacher training, art history, multimedia art.
Summer Programs	6 Weeks: Full Program	Art History, ceramics, drawing, painting, printmaking, sculpture, Undergraduate level	8½ Weeks in each spring and summer on graduate and undergraduate levels
Degree/ Certificate	BA BS—Ind Des MA	BA—4 years BFA—4 years MA—1–2 years MFA—2 years MAT—1–2 years	BFA (1972) BA BS MA MFA (1972)

	MINNESOTA	**NEW YORK**	**OHIO**	
Institution (by state)	**Carleton College**	**Skidmore College**	**The College of Wooster** Department of Art	**Oberlin College** Department of Art
Mailing Address	Northfield, Minnesota 55057	Saratoga Springs, New York 12866	The Department of Art The College of Wooster Wooster, Ohio 44691	Allen Art Building Oberlin, Ohio 44074

	MINNESOTA	NEW YORK	OHIO	
Telephone	(507) 645-4431 Ext 400	(518) 584-5000	(216) 264-1234 Ext 388	(216) 774-1221 Ext 3117
Major Programs	Art history, drawing, printmaking, sculpture, painting.	Art education, painting, sculpture, printmaking, ceramics, design, art history, graphics, weaving, enameling, jewelry and metalwork, serigraphy, textile design, photography, film-making.	History, painting, sculpture, ceramics, graphics, drawing, design, methods of teaching (Art History, Gothic, Byzantine, Renaissance, Baroque, 19th and 20th, African Art, Modern Architecture, etc.)	Painting, sculpture, printmaking, art history, classical archaeology, conservation.
Summer Programs	No Summer Program	6 Weeks	10 Weeks: Art methods and materials	No Summer Program
Degree/ Certificate	BA—4 years	BS Art Ed—4 years BS Studio Art—4 years BA Art Hist—4 years	BA	BA—4 years MA—2 years

Schools whose objectives are consistent with those of the Association but who wish to retain the option of seeking accreditation at a later date.

	PENNSYLVANIA	**DISTRICT OF COLUMBIA**	
Institution (by state)	**Beaver College** Department of Fine Arts	**Corcoran School of Art**	**Howard University** College of Fine Arts Department of Art
Mailing Address	Glenside, Pennsylvania 19038	Seventeenth and New York Ave., N.W. Washington, D.C. 20006	2400 Sixth Street, N.W. Washington, D.C. 20001
Telephone	(215) 884-3500	(202) 628-9484	(202) 636-7047 or 636-7048
Major Programs	Graphic design, interior design, painting, printmaking, art history.	Foundation, fine art, visual communication.	Art education, painting, design, graphics, history of art, sculpture, ceramics, photography, experimental studio.
Summer Programs	No Summer Program	6 Weeks Summer School 4 Weeks School Abroad Leeds College of Art and London, England	6 Weeks: Painting, ceramics, design, drawing, graphics, photography.
Degree/ Certificate	BFA—4 years BA Art History— 4 years	Diploma—4 years	BFA—4 years MFA—2 years MA—2 years

	INDIANA	KENTUCKY	MASSA-CHUSETTS	MICHIGAN
Institution (by state)	Fort Wayne Art Institute School of Fine Arts	Louisville School of Art	Swain School of Design	Art School of the Society of Arts and Crafts
Mailing Address	1026 West Berry Street Fort Wayne, Indiana 46804	100 Park Road Anchorage, Kentucky 40223	19 Hawthorn Street New Bedford, Massachusetts 02740	245 East Kirby Street Detroit, Michigan 48202
Telephone	(219) 743-9796	(502) 245-8836	(617) 997-3158	(313) 872-3118
Major Programs	Painting, sculpture, printmaking, graphic design, ceramics, metalsmithing, art education (in cooperation with Indiana University).	Painting, printmaking, sculpture, ceramics, metalsmithing, textiles, visual communications.	Drawing and painting, graphics, commercial design, illustration and liberal arts.	Painting, sculpture, industrial design, advertising design, ceramics, metalcraft, photography.
Summer Programs	No Summer Program	6 Weeks: Childrens Art, High School Art, Regular Program	8 Weeks: Children and Adults	8 Weeks
Degree/ Certificate	BFA—4 years Certificate—4 years	BFA—4 years Certificate—4 years	BFA—4 years	BFA—8 terms Certificate—8 terms

	MISSOURI	MONTANA	SOUTH DAKOTA
Institution (by state)	Florissant Valley Community College	University of Montana Department of Art	Northern State College Department of Art
Mailing Address	3400 Pershall Road Ferguson, Missouri 63135	Missoula, Montana 59801	Aberdeen, South Dakota 57401
Telephone	(618) 524-2020 Ext. 221	(406) 243-4181	(605) 622-2514
Major Programs	Transfer (Basic first two years of B.F.A.) Commercial Art (Terminal)	Ceramics, sculpture, graphics, design/ crafts, painting.	Creative art, secondary and elementary art teaching, painting, sculpture, ceramics, printmaking, drawing, design, art history, jewelry, crafts.
Summer Programs	6 Weeks 9 Weeks	Summer Program	
Degree/ Certificate	Associate of Arts Associate of Science (Commercial Art)	BA, BFA—4 years MA—1 year MFA—2 years	BA—4 years BS-Ed—4 years MS-Ed—1 year

UNION OF INDEPENDENT COLLEGES OF ART

UICA is a national consortium of nine of the country's strongest and most forward-looking professional colleges of art and design, working together to maximize their strengths and better utilize their resources in cooperative association. Students wishing to apply for admission to more than one UICA school may do so economically and efficiently by utilizing the Mutual Application Program (known, predictably, as MAP).

To apply to more than one UICA school, write to: MAP, 4340 Oak Street, Kansas City, Missouri 64111.

For individual catalogs, write to any of the UICA member institutions:

California College of Arts and Crafts
Broadway at College Avenue
Oakland, California
94618
415-653-8118

Cleveland Institute of Art
11141 East Boulevard
Cleveland, Ohio
44106
216-421-4322

Kansas City Art Institute
4415 Warwick Boulevard
Kansas City, Missouri
64111
316-561-4852

Maryland Institute, College of Art
1300 Mount Royal Avenue
Baltimore, Maryland
21217
301-669-9200

Minneapolis College of Art and Design
200 East 25th Street
Minneapolis, Minnesota
55404
612-339-8905

Philadelphia College of Art
Broad and Pine Streets
Philadelphia, Pennsylvania
19102
215-546-0545

Rhode Island School of Design
Providence, Rhode Island
02903
401-331-3507

San Francisco Art Institute
800 Chestnut Street
San Francisco, California
94133
415-771-7020

School of the Art Institute,
Chicago
Michigan Avenue at Adams Street
Chicago, Illinois
60603
312-236-7080

BIBLIOGRAPHY

BOOKS

Ceramics

Ceramic Design, John B. Kenny (Chilton Book Company, 1970) , $9.95

Ceramics, A Potter's Handbook, Glenn C. Nelson (Holt, Rinehart & Winston, 1971) , $10.95

Clay and Glazes for the Potter, Daniel Rhodes (Chilton Book Company, 1957) , $7.50

Kilns Design, Construction and Operation, Daniel Rhodes (Chilton Book Company, 1971) , $10.00

A Potter's Book, Bernard Leach (Trans Atlantic Arts, 1972) , $12.75

Pottery Step-by-Step, Henry Trevor (Ballantine Books, 1971) , $3.95

Pottery; The Technique of Throwing, John Colbeck (Watson-Guptill, 1971) , $10.00

Step-by-Step Ceramics, Jolyon Hofsted (Golden Press, 1967) , $2.50

The Technique of Handbuilt Pottery, Mollie Winterburn (Watson-Guptill, 1966) , $10.00

Enameling

The Art of Enameling, Margaret Seeler (Van Nostrand Reinhold, 1969) , $14.95

Enameling on Metal, Oppi Untracht (Chilton Book Company, 1971) , $7.50

Experimental Techniques in Enameling, Fred Ball (Van Nostrand Reinhold, 1970) , $7.50

Practical Enameling and Jewelry Work, Brian Newble (Viking, 1967) , $6.95

Simple Enameling, Geoffrey Franklin (Watson-Guptill, 1970) , $7.50

Glass

Glassblowing: A Search for Form, Harvey Littleton (Van Nostrand Reinhold, 1972, $14.95
Glassforming-Glassmaking for the Craftsman, Frederic and Lilli Schuler (Chilton Book Company, 1970), $12.50
Kiln-Fired Glass, Hariette Anderson (Chilton Book Company, 1969), $9.50
Stained Glass Craft, Divine Blatchford (Dover, 1970), $1.50
The Technique of Stained Glass, Patrick Reyntiens (Watson-Guptill, 1972), $15.00

Jewelry

The Design and Creation of Jewelry, Robert von Neumann (Chilton Book Company, 1972), $7.50
Introducing Jewelry Making, John Crawford (Watson-Guptill, 1969), $7.95
Jewelry Form and Technique, Michael D. Grando (Van Nostrand Reinhold, 1969), $5.95
Modern Jewelry Design and Technique, Irena Brynner (Van Nostrand Reinhold, 1969), $10.00
Step-by-Step Jewelry, Thomas Gentille (Golden Press, 1970), $2.50

Macramé

Color and Design in Macramé, Virginia I. Harvey (Van Nostrand Reinhold, 1970), $7.95
Macramé, by Virginia I. Harvey (Van Nostrand Reinhold, 1966), $8.50
Macramé—Creative Design in Knotting, Dona Z. Meilach (Crown Publications, 1970), $3.95
Step-by-Step Macramé, Mary Walker Phillips (Golden Press, 1970), $2.50
Techniques of Rya Knotting, Donald Wilcox (Van Nostrand Reinhold, 1971), $8.95

Textiles

The Art of Weaving, Else Regensteiner (Van Nostrand Reinhold, 1970), $13.50

Byways in Handweaving, Mary M. Atwater (Macmillan, 1972), $8.00

A Handweaver's Pattern Book, Marguerite P. Davison (Davison Books, 1971), $10.00

New Key to Weaving, Mary Black (Macmillan, 1972), $12.00

Step-by-Step Weaving, Nell Znamierowski (Golden Press, 1969), $2.50

The Weaver's Book, Harriet Tidbell (Macmillan, 1971), $6.35

Other Craft Books

Cabinetmaking and Millwork, John L. Feirer (Charles A. Bennett), $12.00

New York Guide to Crafts Supplies, Judith Glassman (Workman Publishing Company, 1972), $2.95

Quilts and Coverlets, Jean Laury (Van Nostrand Reinhold, 1969), $9.95

Woodstock Craftsman's Manual, Jean Young (Praeger, 1972), $4.95

MAGAZINES

Craft Horizons, American Crafts Council, 44 West 53rd Street, New York, New York 10019

Glass Art, Box 7525, Oakland, California 94601

Handweaver and Craftsman, 220 Fifth Avenue, New York, New York 10001

Shuttle, Spindle and Dyepot, Handweavers Guild of America, 1013 Farmington Avenue, West Hartford, Connecticut 06107

Studio Potter, Peter Sabin, Warner, New Hampshire 03278

BOOK SERVICES

Book Barn
P.O. Box 245
Storrs, Connecticut
06268

Herbert Shprentz Company
Box 83
Irvington, New York
10533

The Unicorn
Box 645
Rockville, Maryland
20851

ASSOCIATIONS

Apprenticeship Service Program
Box 908
Montara, California
94037

National Council on Education
for the Ceramic Arts
Fine Arts Building
Room 132
University of Illinois
Champaign, Illinois
61820

Stained Glass Association of
America
c/o Fred Oppleger
822 Wilmington Street
Saint Louis, Missouri
63111

U.S. Potters Association
P.O. Box 63
East Liverpool, Ohio
43920

PART IV

GOING AT CRAFTS ALONE

Craft people are individualists by nature, given to going at crafts alone, private people happy with themselves and their skill. In their work they discover enough substance and communication to sustain themselves. And then, too, creating is a private kind of journey best achieved alone.

The desire to have one's own craft business is strong among many craftsmen. To be able to devote oneself fully to crafts, to form a lifestyle out of the work, is an appealing thought. But this is chancy work and there are many failures, and there are important things to know.

Don't establish your own business, even if it's only throwing pots in your basement, unless you have had some signs of success —if you have been able to sell on consignment (a store owner takes the pieces and pays you only after the pieces have been sold) or you have been successful at art shows or affairs. And selling an odd pot or one piece of metal at a local fair isn't a mark of success. But if criticism of your craft shows that your work has good design, technique, and can be mass-produced at a reasonable price, then go ahead.

If your craft is salable and you're willing to work harder than you would at a regular job, and you don't mind doing "commercial" work, then here's how.

STUDIO/SHOP

You need a working area that's your own. Carve it out of the house, take over the attic, a garage, build a shed. No craft that we can think of requires only a small space. The equipment alone demands room; then there's storage. Perhaps you can rent space, an old barn on a nearby farm, part of a warehouse. What's important in selecting a location is that it's not expensive to rent and is a place where you can work without distraction from people, noise or the weather.

EQUIPMENT/SUPPLIES

Don't get into full-time production with limited equipment and supplies. Make a check list of items you'll need and where you can readily get replacements. It helps in time saved and money spent if you can at least do minor repairs on your equipment. Build up supplies before starting to work. Buy all the equipment you need. It's wise to have the equipment paid for before starting. Don't have a lot of extra bills to pay when you start. Sales will be low for a while, perhaps for a long while, in your business.

PROMOTION

Most craft people we know are shy about their work. They tend to want to stay back and let the objects speak for themselves. That's nice, but it's bad for business. You have to hustle for yourself, promote your craft. Some things to do for yourself:

—Prepare a business card. Use imagination in the creation, color and design. See that the card suggests a serious tone and conveys workmanship.

—Take or have pictures taken of your work, preferably large 8 × 10 glossy photographs of different objects. Also have action shots and slides taken of yourself showing a piece of work at different stages. These slides can be used for television presentations, lectures and demonstrations.

—Prepare an attractive brochure that tells about yourself, where you have studied and with whom (if well known). Have another slip-in card to put in the brochure for information on craft teaching, if you plan on teaching.

—Notify the local newspapers. Write to the editor, department or columnist who handles crafts. Make the letter short, informative and factual. Don't send the letter unless you know the name of the person you want or the section of the newspaper—women's page, travel, Sunday section. Give the newspaper an angle for the story, i.e., you make special pots, your cottage industry is new in town, your enameling is a copy of a historical technique.

—Contact the local television station, the daily talk show, tell them about your studio, say you're available for a demonstration. Offer, for example, to give a lesson on TV, if that's possible.

—Telephone or write as many likely clubs as possible. Offer to give a talk (plus slides) or demonstration of your craft. If you are to appear at a club, write up a brief news release and mail to the newspaper, keep it brief and give only the information: time, place, reason. Make sure you give the paper your full name, telephone and location of business.

—Visit the large shopping centers in your area and offer to put on a craft demonstration. Perhaps you can arrange with other craftsmen to do a variety of crafts over a long weekend. Try to establish a crafts weekend at the centers. Many of the larger shopping malls are already doing this.

—Enter as many local fairs as possible. Plan to spend all your time at these fairs and be prepared with a supply of your finished products. Here's where you meet people!

—Write the craft journals, especially the local regional ones, and keep files of back issues for references.

MARKET PLACE

Another necessary thing to know before beginning your business is your audience. Who are they? Young? Old? Nearly married? Suburbanites? Apartment owners?

An early guess of who they might be would come from the people that purchase your craft at the fairs or in stores. You can gauge the reactions of family and friends—what objects do they like, take an interest in?

If you're a mature and polished crafts person—as you should be before setting up business—you, too, will have made initial decisions about your work. You will have discovered what you want to say with your art and be able to make that statement again and again with each piece. You will have mastered the technique of making this statement in your medium.

Then, beginning to market your craft, you should:

—Prepare an inventory of objects and have several developed lines to sell.

—Prepare a presentation book of your objects, well illustrated with color pictures. Have a price list with all facts: sizes, prizes, variety.

—Prepare an accounting system. Do this yourself or get help. Also a system for billing customers.

—Have a letterhead done with your business name and address.

RETAIL/WHOLESALE

Opening your own store requires a great deal of additional work and experience and should not be attempted alone. It just takes too much time away from your craft. And if you are selling just your craft, or say, just pottery, the market is too narrow to make it in a retail store. About the only way you can make it is to have a "floating" sidewalk stall, some way to cut down overhead expenses.

It is easier to develop a business by wholesaling your goods. Here are some preliminary steps you might consider taking:

—Obtain a mailing list of craft shops. The American Crafts Council (44 West 53rd Street, New York, New York 10019) has such a list for sale. Send out a mailing of your brochure, price list. You can expect about a four percent return on this system.

—Visit the shops in your immediate area. Leave information with them if they aren't interested in buying at the moment. Next go to the larger department stores in town. Fill these orders. Make sure you can meet deadlines before expanding further.

—Hire a salesman. Hire more than one salesman. Arrange it so that each has a territory. Make sure he isn't just taking you on as a sideline to other and more important business. Get a salesman who is selling goods that are complementary to your work. Begin slowly, hire one salesman at a time and test him or her out first. Also, don't hire someone unless you have checked out the references.

Plan on giving this salesman between fifteen and twenty percent of your order. Write a contract out so the territory and terms are clear. You can find salesmen by asking gift shop proprietors whom they see. Check the classified ads in trade magazines. In larger cities there will be marketing centers, regional offices of national distributors. Shop around first.

A salesman (and/or company) will want to know the following:

> prices
> sizes and designs
> method of packing and shipping
> availability of discounts

They will also want to know how serious you are about this business. They will not want to take you on unless they can count on your producing and being with them for several years.

—In time it will be possible to arrange with a wholesale distributor. A wholesale distributor operates as a middle-man between you and the retailer. He buys your craft out-right at a discount of thirty-three percent of the wholesale price. That's a lot but you have your payment immediately, you deliver to only one location, no more worries about packing, and it cuts down on all additional bookkeeping. You normally sell all your goods to the distributor.

SUBCONTRACTORS

Soon after you're in full operation you'll find you need to subcontract. Your business will be growing too rapidly to keep up. One way of "subcontracting" is getting an apprentice. You teach this person the craft and he works for you. These arrangements—from a business viewpoint—are chancy.

It's best to find people who can do bits of your work and train them for part-time, but long-time employment. Break down your craft and see what parts you alone can do and want to do, the parts that give you the most enjoyment. You will still be required to train and organize the people you hire. Pick your employees carefully. Also try to establish these pieceworkers elsewhere than on your own premises, as in a cottage industry. You then will have more space in your own studio. Some suggestions:

—Pay by the piece, not the hour.

—Clearly define the tasks to be done and train only for that.

—Set deadlines for your workers.

—Select people who will be with you for a while, and people who like the work.

BUSINESS ASPECTS

There are other important considerations of a non-craft nature that need to be handled professionally, either by you or someone you hire. Some are:

—Keeping books. This is a necessity, especially if you're dealing with a payroll, plus a salesman, plus direct mail. You need a system of records from the very first day. Get good at this or hire someone!

—Selling and work permits. Check on your local regulations, contact the Small Business Administration.

—What is taxable? This can be a big help, really, in saving you money. But you must:

—keep records of your expenses

—open a separate bank account for your business

—prove that you're in business to make a profit.

There are many deductions that you can claim: postage, stationery, supplies, equipment, commissions, professional magazines, etc. Remember, you're in business.

Before beginning, get these books and publications. You can learn a lot from them.

Craft Shops: USA
American Crafts Council
44 West 53rd Street
New York, New York
10019

Developing "Home-grown"
Industry
Department of Commerce
Obtain from:
U.S. Government Printing Office
Washington, D.C.
20402

Gift and Art Shop
John W. Robinson
Small Business Bibliography
No. 26
Small Business Administration
Washington, D.C.
20416

The Handcraft Business
Vol. 10, No. 8
Small Business Reporter
Bank of America
P.O. Box 37000
San Francisco, California
94137

Handicrafts and Home Business
Small Business Bibliography
Revised No. 1
Small Business Administration
Washington, D.C.
20416

How to Sell Your Handicrafts
Robert G. Hart
David McKay Co. Inc.
New York, New York
10017

Selling Your Crafts
Norbert N. Nelson
Reinhold Publishing Company
430 Park Avenue
New York, New York
10022

Selling by Mail Order
Reprint December 1969, No. 3
Small Business Administration
Washington, D.C.
20416

Specialized Help for Small
Business
David R. Mayne
Small Marketers Aids No. 74
Small Business Administration
Washington, D.C.
20416

Tax Guide for Small Business
Publication 334
Department of the Treasury
Obtain from:
U.S. Government Printing Office
Washington, D.C.
20402

Taxes and the Craftsman
Sydney Prerau
American Craftsmen's Council
New York, New York
10019

HANDCRAFTS, INC.

When craftsmen collect, they collect among themselves. This is perhaps the best reason for a group of like souls to establish a craft cooperative. A cooperative is simply a business organization. It can help a group of craftsmen sell their products, buy supplies, provide training for others. It is a way for people to make a living working in crafts where otherwise they would not be able to succeed. It's as simple as that. Also, it has the extra advantage of bringing together people who share a common desire about crafts and perhaps also share a common lifestyle.

Perhaps no one in America has done more thinking about craft cooperatives than economist William R. Seymour of the Farmer Cooperative Service of the Department of Agriculture. Seymour has outlined what makes a crafts (or any) cooperative different. There are three points:

First, a cooperative is different from a business firm in the way it handles its receipts. In most cooperatives, the net margin over the cost of operations is returned to the patrons who have used the cooperative. The return is in proportion to his use of the cooperative.

Second, it differs from other types of business firms in its source of control. Investor-oriented corporations are controlled by stockholder investors. These may or may not be its users or customers. A cooperative on the other hand, is owned and controlled by its member-patrons.

Third, a cooperative is organized to serve the needs of its members, whereas other commercial firms are organized to earn profits and returns on invested capital.

The study that has gone into cooperatives has produced some basic principles that must be observed if there is to be any chance of success. Much of this information is obtainable in a series of pamphlets published by the Department of Agriculture, but this is what you should know before beginning a cooperative.

FEASIBILITY STUDY

Some sort of feasibility study (however informal) should take place. This is to give you information about the economic factors and the individuals involved. You should know the following:

—Do members understand what a cooperative is?

—Why are they joining?

—How large is the membership?

—Do you have among the people involved leadership and management skills?

—What benefits are to be gained by the cooperative?

—What is the competition for this particular craft product?

If the answers to these questions are positive, then there is a set of principles that make a successful cooperative. They are, briefly:

—Training of members—not only in production to gain the volume needed, but also in cooperative principles and organization.

—Quality control of products.

—Establish market outlets.

—Produce to specification of processors or consumers.

—Hold fixed and variable cost to a minimum.

—Contract for every service possible.

—Be prepared to meet competition.

—Select a capable manager.

—Keep accurate financial records.

—Business operation should be reviewed carefully by the board of directors.

—Audit and business analysis at the end of the year.

—Develop a sound and realistic budget and operate in accordance therewith.

—Establish and maintain the required account.

These principles break down into six different areas when it comes to practice. They are:

Product

—The quality of the product and the skill required to make it must be sufficient to assure its sale for a good price so that the worker will receive a minimum wage, or higher, for his work.

—The product should be one for which a continued demand can be reasonably assured.

Production

—There must be physical facilities and equipment that are necessary for production, or a feasible plan to provide them.

—The methods of production must be efficient and appropriate to the particular craft. Mechanized equipment and machines and processed raw materials may be used to promote efficiency as long as production methods allow a substantial and effective role for both human skills and individual expression in achieving the unique quality characteristic of handcraft.

Marketing

—The project should include marketing plans, based on knowledge of the existing demand for the product in question, and a reasonable assurance of potential sales. Means of marketing the product should have been arranged with a wholesaler, jobber, or several retail outlets. If the group is to open its own outlet a market study must be made to determine the best location, the variety and quantity needed to efficiently operate; and how it is to be initially (one year) financed. Also, how will it be financed from the second to fifth years.

Training

—There must be provision for a training program of sufficient duration to develop craftsmen with skills adequate to maintain the quality of the product as well as to guarantee a continuous supply of sufficient quantity.

Personnel

—The importance of the following personnel can't be overlooked.

a. A skilled designer-craftsman who will furnish prototypes of superior quality and assure design flexibility.
b. A person skilled in management and production unless the designer-craftsman has proven ability in this area.
c. Adequate personnel to handle administrative matters.
d. A person, who may or may not be the designer-craftsman, who possesses the sufficient knowledge and skills to train the craftsmen to be employed in the enterprise. This person should be knowledgeable in cooperative practices and principles.

Location

—Since a craft project should be evaluated like any other business enterprise, the question of location should be considered.

a. The project should be welcomed by the community.
b. There should be evidence that there is sufficient interest in the products.
c. There should be an availability of raw materials locally or within easy reach.
d. Tourists and recreation programs emphasizing the cultural uniqueness of the region would be advantageous.

COOPERATIVE STRUCTURE

There are several different models of craft structures, but for our purposes the only interesting one is the local cooperative

organization. William R. Seymour in his fine publication for the Farmer Cooperative Service, *American Crafts: A Rich Heritage and a Rich Future,* has listed the advantages of a local cooperative:
—Members know each other;
—All members have the same marketing and production problems that create a unity of interest;
—The business is usually easily understood and conducted by the craftsmen;
—Members usually have confidence in the local manager who knows them and meets with them regularly;
—It is an effective medium for extending marketing and production information to the members;
—The association is the basis for establishing a federated organization.
Membership for this local cooperative organization can be arranged several ways: purchasing a share of stock, membership certificate and/or by signing a marketing contract.

STARTING A COOPERATIVE

Cooperatives, like almost anything else, start when a few committed people have a problem and get together to solve it. The first steps they take are to find out the legal implications and to get hold of the basic readings on cooperatives. Some states have specific laws for non-agriculture cooperatives under which craft cooperatives can incorporate. In some cases, it may be more feasible to incorporate under the regular incorporation law of the state and set up bylaws so as to operate as a cooperative.

Other groups may elect to incorporate in the District of Columbia under Public Law No. 642–76, Congress, Chapter 397–30, Session S. 2013 and then incorporate in their state as an out-of-state cooperation.

At this point it is time to get technical assistance. The initial contact should be with your local extension agent. If he is unfamiliar with crafts and/or cooperatives he can call upon the professional staff at the state land grant university. Other sources of help could be an established cooperative, state cooperative council, county office of Farmers Home Administration, Production Credit Association or District Bank for Cooperatives.

Next, call a meeting. Make sure:

—Date, time and place are convenient for all possible members.

—Prepare careful presentation; an adviser could be helpful here.

—Establish a survey committee, with business ability, to make a detailed study of the craft cooperative possibilities.

—Do not force anyone to commit himself to becoming a member. Do not set any cooperative policies.

The survey team needs to make two decisions: (1) judge whether the proposed cooperative is likely to be successful; (2) and if so, work out the preliminary organization pattern for the business. The areas the committee must explore are: need for the cooperative; potential membership and potential volume of business; management skills needed; facilities needed; operating costs; capitalization; and legal requirements.

Another meeting of potential members is then needed to review the survey report and establish an organization committee. The organization committee should contain some of all of the survey committee. The organization committee has five main jobs: (1) sign up the required number of members; (2) obtain the capital subscribed and arrange for capital loans; (3) draft the legal organization papers; (4) file the articles of incorporation; (5) arrange the first membership meeting.

(Help on drafting the legal organization papers can be obtained in pamphlet form from the Farmer Cooperative Service. The address is: U.S. Department of Agriculture, Washington, D.C. 20250.)

Management of the cooperative is the key to success of the organization. It is up to the members themselves to see that the management works. Members, according to William R. Seymour, "should be intimately and personally involved in the affairs of their cooperative and should have a positive role in its management."

Some of the more important management responsibilities of the members:

—Adopting and amending bylaws and articles of incorporation.

—Approving major changes in operation and substantial income expenditures.

—Electing a competent board of directors.

—Studying issues and keeping the board informed of their desires.

The board of directors must be cooperative members, elected by the other members. They represent members as users of cooperative services, not as capital investors, a unique feature of cooperative organization. They hold the key position between producer-members and hired management.

The hired management in a cooperative includes the manager as well as other key personnel who are given management functions. The manager has as his or her responsibility, the following:

—operating the business

—establishing goals

—developing the work schedule

—directing quality control

In establishing the structure of the cooperative it is important to reply on the experience of such national organizations as the Farmer Cooperative Service. Their information is published in bureaucratic forms but written in simple English, and the information is all there, once you get by the cartoons.

REACHING THE PUBLIC

Craft cooperatives are rather new. They have begun to flourish mainly in low-income communities, with the help of federal monies. Also many communities in the South over the years have had co-ops that usually involved the women of the town.

Craft cooperatives or groups who share a love for pottery or weaving can be successful. After the bylaws are written and the association formed, get yourself known. Some ways to do this:

—Contact the local newspapers, tell them about your new

cooperative. Keep the paper informed of meetings and development.

—Write the craft journals, regional and national. Try to get a story done about yourselves.

—Get on the local television station, on the noontime talk show. Offer to do a demonstration, show slides.

—Contact the large shopping malls and see if you can put on a weekend show, a mini-fair.

—If you're in a rural community buy outdoor advertising. It's inexpensive.

WHY COOPERATIVES?

All of this seems like a lot of work, too much work, and it is, but there are advantages:

—low costs for supplies: ability to buy in quantity

—technical assistance: training for each other and new members

—new designs and products: members contribute new ideas for consideration by the membership

—marketing: a manager can take over the responsibility of selling for the group; he or she can sell full time

—efficient business operation: clerical help (either hired or one of the members) can keep the records for the cooperative

—joint use of equipment: in some crafts it's possible to share equipment, buy new equipment together

If you go ahead, here are sources of additional information:

Publications

A Handbook and Resource Guide for New Craft Groups, July 1970
The Commission on Religion in Appalachia, Inc.
864 Weisgarber Road
Knoxville, Tennessee
37919
(cost $1.00)

Handicrafts and Home Businesses
Reprint March 1970, No. 1

Small Business Administration
Washington, D.C.
20416

Selling by Mail Order
Reprint December 1969, No. 3
Small Business Administration
Washington, D.C.
20416
(single copies free)

Information on particular steps in the cooperative-forming process is contained in publications of the Farmer Cooperative Service. Single copies of the publications listed below may be obtained free by writing Publications, Farmer Cooperative Service, U.S. Department of Agriculture, Washington, D.C. 20250.

American Crafts: A Rich Heritage and a Rich Future—FCS Program Aid No. 1026. William R. Seymour

The Cooperative Approach to Crafts—Program Aid No. 1001. William R. Seymour

Cooperatives—Distinctive Business Corporations—FCS Information 65. C. H. Kirkman, Jr.

Cooperatives in the American Private Enterprise System—Educational Aid 5. C. H. Kirkman, Jr.

Co-ops—A Tool to Improve and Market Crafts—Reprint 363 from "News for Farmer Cooperatives"

How to Start a Cooperative—Educational Circular 18. Irwin W. Rust

Is There a Co-op in Your Future—FCS Information 81. C. H. Kirkman, Jr.

Manager Holds an Important Key to Co-op Success—FCS Information 74. C. H. Kirkman, Jr.

Members Make Co-ops Go—FCS Information 72. C. H. Kirkman, Jr.

Sample Legal Documents: Legal Phases of Farmer Cooperatives—FCS Information 66

What Are Cooperatives—FCS Information 67. C. H. Kirkman, Jr.

Agencies

American Crafts Council
44 W. 53rd Street
New York, New York
10019

American Federation of Arts
41 East 65th Street
New York, New York
10021

Appalachian Regional Commission
1666 Connecticut Avenue, N.W.
Washington, D.C.
20251

Associated Councils of Art
1564 Broadway
New York, New York
10036

Southern Highland Handicraft Guild
P.O. Box 9145, 15 Reddick Road
Asheville, North Carolina
28805

Farmer Cooperative Extension Service

Alabama
Auburn University
Auburn, Alabama
36830
205-826-4444

Alaska
University of Alaska
College, Alaska
99701
907-479-7259

Arizona
University of Arizona
Tucson, Arizona
85721
602-884-2711

Arkansas
P.O. Box 391
Little Rock, Arkansas
72203
501-376-6301

California
University of California
2200 University Avenue
Berkeley, California
94720
415-642-7252

Colorado
Colorado State University
Fort Collins, Colorado
80521
301-491-6281

Connecticut
University of Connecticut
Storrs, Connecticut
06268
203-429-3311, Ext. 238

Delaware
University of Delaware
Newark, Delaware
19711
302-738-2504

District of Columbia
Federal City College
1424 K St., N.W.
Washington, D.C.
20006
202-638-4726

Florida
University of Florida
Gainesville, Florida
32601
904-392-1761

Georgia
University of Georgia
Athens, Georgia
30601
404-542-3824

Hawaii
University of Hawaii
Honolulu, Hawaii
96822
808-944-8234

Idaho
University of Idaho
Moscow, Idaho
83843
208-885-6151

Illinois
University of Illinois
Urbana, Illinois
61801
217-333-2660

Indiana
Purdue University
Lafayette, Indiana
47907
317-749-2413

Iowa
Iowa State University
Ames, Iowa
50010
515-294-4576

Kansas
Kansas State University
Manhattan, Kansas
66502
913-532-5820

Kentucky
University of Kentucky
Lexington, Kentucky
40506
606-257-4772

Louisiana
Louisiana State University
Baton Rouge, Louisiana
70803
504-343-7444

Maine
University of Maine
Orono, Maine
04473
207-581-7200

Maryland
University of Maryland
College Park, Maryland
20742
301-454-3742

Massachusetts
University of Massachusetts
Amherst, Massachusetts
01002
413-545-2766

Michigan
Michigan State University
East Lansing, Michigan
48823
517-355-2308

Minnesota
University of Minnesota
St. Paul, Minnesota
55101
612-373-1223

Mississippi
Mississippi State University
State College, Mississippi
39762
601-325-4436

Missouri
University of Missouri
309 University Hall
Columbia, Missouri
65201
314-449-8186

Montana
Montana State University
Bozeman, Montana
59715
406-587-3121, Ext. 271

Nebraska
University of Nebraska
Lincoln, Nebraska
68503
402-472-7211, Ext. 2966

Nevada
University of Nevada
Reno, Nevada
89507
702-784-6611

New Hampshire
University of New Hampshire
Durham, New Hampshire
03824
603-862-1520

New Jersey
Rutgers—The State University
P.O. Box 231
New Brunswick, New Jersey
08903
201-247-1766, Ext. 1306

New Mexico
New Mexico State University
Las Cruces, New Mexico
88001
505-646-1806

New York
State College of Agriculture
Ithaca, New York
14850
607-256-2117

North Carolina
North Carolina State University
Raleigh, North Carolina
27607
919-755-2812

North Dakota
North Dakota State University
Fargo, North Dakota
58102
701-237-8944

Ohio
Ohio State University
2120 Fyffe Road
Columbus, Ohio
43210
614-422-6891

Oklahoma
Oklahoma State University
Stillwater, Oklahoma
74074
405-372-6211, Ext. 212

Oregon
Oregon State University
Corvallis, Oregon
97331
503-754-2713

Pennsylvania
Pennsylvania State University
University Park, Pennsylvania
16802
814-865-2541

Puerto Rico
University of Puerto Rico
Rio Piedras, Puerto Rico
00928
809-765-8000

Rhode Island
University of Rhode Island
Kingston, Rhode Island
02881
401-792-2476

South Carolina
Clemson University
Clemson, South Carolina
29631
803-656-3382

South Dakota
South Dakota State University
Brookings, South Dakota
57006
605-688-4147

Tennessee
University of Tennessee
P.O. Box 1071
Knoxville, Tennessee
37901
615-974-7114

Texas
Texas A.&M. University
College Station, Texas
77843
713-845-6411, Ext. 268

Utah
Utah State University
Logan, Utah
84321
801-752-4100, Ext. 268

Vermont
University of Vermont
Burlington, Vermont
05401
802-656-2990

Virgin Islands
P.O. Box 166
Kingshill
St. Croix, Virgin Islands
00850
809-773-0246

Virginia
Virginia Polytechnic Institute
Blacksburg, Virginia
24061
703-552-6705

Washington
Washington State University
Pullman, Washington
99163
509-335-7205

West Virginia
West Virginia University
294 Coliseum
Morgantown, West Virginia
26505
304-293-5691

Wisconsin
University of Wisconsin
432 North Lake Street
Madison, Wisconsin
53706
608-262-3786

Wyoming
University of Wyoming
Box 3354, University Station
Laramie, Wyoming
82070
307-766-3253

CRAFTS UTOPIA

The third possibility for developing a craft organization is the commune, an intentional community best defined (loosely) as a close living, cohesive, largely self-supporting group of people, whose communal life is fairly all-inclusive of its members needs. The grouping is voluntary, and the group's culture is self-formulated.

There is nothing new about communal living in America. The first such community were the Shakers, who were "separatists, experimenters, seekers after a more spiritual life" who formed their organization in 1790 in Pittsfield, Massachusetts.

Lately—really within the last five years—communes have been seized upon as a new way of living, mostly among middle-class sons and daughters of suburban parents. As one member wrote in *Alternatives Newsletter* early in 1971, "I can sometimes imagine a landscape of small communes, self-supportive and independent, but interlocked in a system of over-government whose principal function is advisory, coordinative, and mediatory; . . . Within these myriad communes, people are free to pursue happiness each in his own peculiar manner, secure nonetheless in the company of his fellows."

From the hopeful wishes of this member some serious study of communal living has been in progress. Last year Kathleen Kinkade of the successful Twin Oaks community wrote *A Walden Two Experiment: The First Five Years of Twin Oaks Community,* a personal history of how this Richmond, Virginia, community is run on lines laid down by B. F. Skinner in his utopian novel *Walden Two.*

More recently Judson Jerome completed a study of the contemporary commune movement. Jerome, a poet, novelist, and

teacher, now lives on a farming commune in Pennsylvania. He
has written brilliantly of what he calls the New Age, a revolution
in consciousness and a redefinition of personhood and wealth and
of the relation of humanity to nature. For the future he sees:

> Everywhere around the country new communities are
> forming for mutual education, to build an ethos that can hold
> people, a nation, a planet, together; something which tran-
> scends the trappings of hippie styles, astrological dilettantism,
> adolescent rebelliousness, and drug revelations. It is not a
> rejection of our heritage but a revival—essentially a religious
> revival—of its most vital elements, grown sooty in an age of
> industrialism which is now passing. I call it the revolution of
> alternative rewards. Can we now begin asking ourselves what
> we really want and how we can get it? Not power, surely, nor
> the illusory security of accumulated possessions, of status, of
> tinsel, and of neon success. Like people everywhere, we want—
> if we can only remember—things simple and abundant, such as
> love. Can sex become an automobile-substitute? Can potatoes
> replace potato chips? Can our civilization, with all its wealth
> and ingenuity, supply us with clean air and blue water? Or are
> we doomed, like a modern King Midas, to turn everything we
> touch into plastic?—*The Annals of The American Academy
> of Political and Social Science,* November, 1972.

Craftsmen, if they want to do anything, want to keep the
world from becoming plastic. And communal craftsmen—with
the Shakers of Pittsfield, Massachusetts—had a sound beginning.
The Shakers, in fact, were our greatest community of craftsmen.

"All things," according to Joseph Meacham, the first male
leader of the Shakers, "must be made according to their order
and use." Adhering to a code that emphasized function and for-
bidding anything "fancy" or "vain," the joiners created a distinctive school of craftsmanship in their chairs, tables, beds, chests
of drawers, their buildings.

According to artist Charles Sheeler, "they recognized no
justifiable difference to be made in the quality of workmanship
for any object, no gradation in the importance of the task. All
must be done equally well." And always they followed this rule
in what they built: "Let it be plain and simple of good and sub-

stantial quality, unembellished by any superfluities which add nothing to its goodness or durability."

The Shakers were able to achieve this quality of craftsmenship through the advantages of cooperative labor. Edward Deming Andrews writing about the Shaker communities said:

> There was, of necessity, routine and system in the day's work: they rose, ate, worked, held meetings and retired at specific hours. But they also believed in variety and division of labor. The sisters took turns ("tours") in the kitchen, laundry, dairy, weave shops, nurse shops, and in household duties. Seasonal market demands, weather conditions and other factors determined the work of the brethren, who, possessed as they often were of several skills, were often shifted from one occupation to another. All labored, but no one was overworked. Visitors often noted the peaceful tempo of Shaker life, as though every day were the Sabbath.

Janet Malcolm, in an article in *The New Yorker*, March 3, 1973, pointed out that "Shaker furniture was made for and used by Shakers" and that was the most important element of their designs. "The gaunt, strange beauty of proportion," she writes, "that marks Shaker furniture and makes it unlike any other furniture arose from the needs of communal life . . . they take their design from specialized cooperative purposes in just the way that the forms within hives follow the specialized functions of the bees."

The craft achievements of the Shakers were also based on an understanding of the "realities" of the world. "From the outset," wrote Edward Deming Andrews, "the Shaker objective was a large measure of self-sufficiency, in food, clothing and shelter; but they were realistic enough to know that a good life, as well as the development of their communities and the advancement of the cause, required income and capital which could only come from commerce with the world."

In a book published in 1905, Eldress Anna White and Leila S. Taylor—both Shakers—wrote, "The Shaker is by no means a dreamer or a mystic. Hardheaded, shrewd, sensible and practical, he neither cheats nor means to let himself be cheated. He sees no virtue nor economy in hard labor when consecrated brain can work out an easier method—and thus the world is rich for many tangible proofs of the Shakers' consecrated ingenuity."

The list of inventions is long and among them were: a flat broom and a machine for sizing broom-corn brush, an improved washing machine, the common clothes pin, the circular saw, metal pins, the one-horse wagon, a sidehill plow, pipe machine, pea sheller, butter worker, looms for weaving palm leaf (for bonnets), a silk-reeling machine, an apple parer, and machines for threshing and fertilizing, machines for matching boards, planing, splint-making and basketry, and so forth.

The Shakers have been one of the most durable utopian communities, despite the fact that celibacy is one of their tenets. At the height of their development, just before the Civil War, they had a total membership of eighteen societies and about 6,000 members. Today less than a dozen—all women—are alive.

The Shakers proved, and to a certain degree so did the Oneida community with their silverware, that beautifully crafted items could be made communally and by production methods. Edward Deming Andrews in his classic book *Shaker Furniture* explains in part how the production methods were achieved without loss of creativity.

> The system of rotation and change in occupation affected the quality of workmanship in several ways. Since no one, with the possible exception of the chair-maker, confined his attention to a single pursuit, it was easier to follow the established tradition of simple design than to experiment with more difficult forms. The more skillful joiners, in particular, were called upon to such a multitude of jobs that the most direct and economical method of finishing a given piece of furniture was also the most practical one. Variety in industry, on the other hand militated against stereotyped performance: the joiner did not make one case of drawers or bed after another, but approached each project freshly from some other calling. Production was always for use; work was incessant but seldom hurried. Emergencies rarely existed and he could choose his own time to finish the work at hand. The craftsman labored neither for master nor market demand, but for a community

which he believed would be timeless. Pursuing the millennial ideal of mutual helpfulness, woodworkers also went from house to house, from family to family, and often from one society to another. They borrowed freely what was best in each community, and thus helped to preserve the highest standards of craftsmanship.*

What was essential to the Shakers' success was their code of living, their purpose in life. Such ingredients today, outside of religious communities, are difficult to find. People coming together today in this new surge of interest for a communal lifestyle are seeking the advantages of extended family living—many communities are only six or eight people, and twelve appears to be the ideal number—where they can obtain close relationships with people. They are not seeking excellence, for example, in some community product, some craft. Such crafts and products made for sale by communes tend to be semi-tooled and lacking in sophistication. The loose democracy of these collectives usually means a lowering of standards—a notable exception would be the hammocks made by Twin Oaks—partly because people in communes resist certain forms of "professionalism," see it as a sign and sin of the outside culture; partly because the individuals in the community who are artists need to lower their standards of achievement for a craft item so as to involve in production other members of the commune who do not have the skills or inclinations toward crafted objects.

The craftsman in the collective faces a dilemma. He can "protect" his craft from the community, keep it personal and creative, but such action then separates him from the community. Communals are not built around individual ego trips. The Shakers shifted members from one occupation to another if the member took "too vain a pride in his work." Or the craftsman can form a commune around the production of a particular craft or crafts. He or she can join a communal situation where the quality of workmanship is to a large part the reason for the community.

---

* Edward Deming Andrews, *Shaker Furniture* (Dover Publication, 1937, 1964).

There are communal arrangements where people work on their individual craft, one-of-a-kind pieces, and share certain aspects of the extended family relationships, but to our knowledge there are no intentional or experimental communities that have attempted to achieve what the Shakers first had in Massachusetts.

What if a small group of craftsmen decided to organize an intentional community around the production of quality handcrafted products? A communal situation that would give them the advantages of the extended family, a lifestyle of their own, and income from their crafted goods?

Much has been written about the communal movement; its trials and errors and successes. The best sources of such information have been the publications of the Alternatives Foundation, particularly their *Modern Utopian* books, and recently the new magazine of the communities, *Communities*. Anyone interested in establishing a crafts community should do the readings of the movement. Additionally, there are other questions to be considered before beginning.

Purpose: The reason for the crafts community has to be defined and agreed upon, written down and comprehended. The most basic of all decisions is what product will be produced—furniture, ceramics, leather?—however, the skills of the founders will solve this question. And rightly so.

Individual Expectations: The expectations of individual craftsmen joining the community must be in line with the purpose of the community as a whole. This is very important: can the craftsmen share in the production of the crafted items?

Apprenticeships: How to train people within the community to do the skilled labor needed for production is not an insurmountable problem. The Shakers solved it for themselves; they were continually getting young boys and girls into the community, orphans and wards of the state. These orphans were trained in specific areas. In Hervey Elkins' book, *Fifteen Years in the Senior Order of Shakers,* he tells about one day's work of an apprentice:

> One of the pupils, a youth of fourteen years of age, made three wood boxes; one of a large size, the sides being fastened

together with joists and spikes; the others designed for the furnishing of dwelling rooms, were made nice, being fitted · together in the manner of a reversed wedge, or (in carpenter's language) dovetailed: bottomed two chairs with flag; one with woven strands; covering eight or ten with leather; made four pairs leather mittens; seven pairs gloves; twenty axe helves; and split and drew the wood for the family laundry.

Today in northeastern Tennessee a successful training program by an Appalachian company is operating in the making of Iron Mountain stoneware. The plant hires the chronically unemployed in the area, has an intensive ten-week program, where working with clay is the most important segment, and hires the best potters. Of the sixteen workers first selected ten are still with Iron Mountain eight years after starting.

Any craft community would have to realize that training new members is necessary for the strength and growth of the commune, and plan accordingly.

Basic Agreements: Once the general purpose and expectations have been defined, additional agreements must be reached. These are the hard, everyday, practical agreements of the society. These, too, should be written down and remembered. Some of the specific agreements are:

—money: how is it to be collected and spent

—child rearing: the community needs to make two decisions: (1) whether to have children; (2) how are they raised, i.e., how permissive or authoritarian, type of school, etc.

—sex: strict monogamy, complete freedom, how much of a limit

—living situations: separate housing, dormitories, etc.

—possessions: what to hold in common, what is private property, if any

—work responsibilities: who does the maintenance tasks and how

—visitor policy: how open a community, how necessary a system for privacy

—drugs: decisions on use, if any

—neighbor policy: relations with immediate outside community

As the community changes these agreements will be altered, but new agreements should be understood by all and agreed to by everyone.

Establishing the Community: The physical heart of the community is the land and buildings. How the land is "held" is another key decision for the group. The three alternatives in buying community property are:

—one person owns it

—everyone owns it

—a society is formed which will own it

The last alternative is the best way: a non-profit corporation. A corporation can be established for about $200 and a board of directors is then elected from the members; everyone has a say in the operation of the community. Such a legal structure permits tax benefits and allows for a smoother business operation with regard to the craft production. In developing the business side of the commune the suggestions given in the section "Handcrafts, Inc." can be adapted for the community organization.

One problem! While publicity is good for business it hurts the commune itself. Try to separate the two aspects of the society. For example, if you decide on a retail store then locate it away from the commune itself. Intentional communities need as much privacy as they can get.

Expansion: The success of the community will be to a large degree based on the solidarity of the core members who conceived the idea. But even those members may leave the commune. Less than half of the original members of Twin Oaks are still there, six years after they began. So new members are needed, though the community in one sense becomes a new community each time a member is added or lost. The core group should also add new members, and in such a way it keeps its strength and the solidarity required to maintain the idea itself.

FINAL NOTE

The decision to form a community around a craft (or crafts) is only part of the idea of a commune situation. Years ago a Canadian commune wrote a booklet published in the *Alternatives*

Newsletter, about the organization of a community. In it they said, "Making a community is making a lifestyle; taking responsibility for your life in your own hands. Like any major human undertaking, it requires courage, the solidity of character that comes from being on friendly terms with yourself, limitless patience and occasional heroism. But the rewards are great in accordance with the sacrifices. You will learn a great deal about yourself and about people, and grow in proportion to your willingness to suffer for love. And it's a very exciting game to play." By seeking a crafts utopia you follow your desires to be creative in handcrafted work while at the same time committing yourself into the life of an extended family.

Source of Information

Alternatives Journal, a directory-in-process, available at $5 a year by writing to Richard Fairfield, P.O. Box 36604, Los Angeles, California 90036.

Communities, a magazine published by five communal groups, available at $6 a year by writing Community Publications Cooperative, P.O. Drawer 426, Louisa, Virginia 23093.

Homesteader is the bimonthly paper of the Christian Homesteading Movement, available for $1 the first year and 50¢ each year thereafter by writing RD 2, Oxford, New York, 13830. The Christian Homesteading Movement also has a Homesteading Center. Its purpose is to prepare members of CHM for community life, with short intensive training periods. The Homesteading Center is also a resource center for members in getting them started in subsistence farming. They describe themselves "as a homesteading school for adults or as a training and experimental farm." Their motto is: A Horse in Every Barn.

North American Student Cooperative Organization is a clearinghouse for information on co-op enterprises, communities, and community-oriented activities through a bi-weekly newsletter, the *New Harbinger,* available at $6 a year by writing NASCO, 1500 Gilbert Court, Ann Arbor, Michigan 48105.

ABOUT THE AUTHORS

JOHN COYNE holds degrees in English from Saint Louis University and Western Michigan University. For five years he was with the Peace Corps, working in Ethiopia and Washington, D.C. For two years he was Director of Student Services and International Education at the State University of New York, Old Westbury. He has written or edited six books and lives in Washington, D.C., and Menorca, Spain.

TOM HEBERT is from Vashon Island in Puget Sound. He studied at Linfield College in Oregon, University of Washington, University of Guanajuato, Mexico, Dallas Theatre Center, Baylor University and UCLA. He taught at Prairie View A & M in Texas and the University of Ibadan, Nigeria. From 1966 to 1968 he lived in Vietnam. In 1968 he joined UNICEF as a Refugee Relief Officer in the Biafran War. An educational writer, he has done studies for the State University of New York, Antioch College, foundations and the Peace Corps. Mr. Hebert longs to have a small hotel in the Caribbean. He lives in Washington, D.C.